The Wisdom
of
His Word

"Lessons in Living as Revealed by the Holy Sprit"

by

Betty Jorgensen Carr

PUBLISHED IN THE UNITED STATES OF AMERICA
BY
BLACK FOREST PRESS
539 TELEGRAPH CANYON ROAD
P.O. BOX 521
CHULA VISTA, CA 91910
(619) 656-8048

Printed in the United States of America
Library of Congress
Cataloging-in- Publication

ISBN: 1-881116-79-4
Copyright © AUGUST, 1996 By Betty Jorgenson Carr

CONTENTS

SECTION ONE

HOW WE HANDLE THE PROBLEMS WE FACE

SECTION TWO

HOW WE TURN THINGS OVER TO GOD

SECTION THREE

KNOW YOUR WEAPONS

SECTION FOUR

LET THE OLD NATURE DIE

SECTION FIVE

FAITH AND HEALING

SECTION SIX

INSIGHTS INTO CHRISTIAN LIVING

DEDICATION

My sister, Doris Cobley, who has faithfully prayed for me and to Peggy Eckstein and Pastor Wm. Gorrell, both of whom encouraged me, taught me and helped me on the Christian road.

ACKNOWLEDGEMENTS

Vernell Davis for her support and her expertise in editing. Barbara Perrier, for allowing her picture "the Pentecost" to be used as our book cover.

Sheila and Arthur Rose, Ken Volz and June Schlunegger who are my faithful prayer warriors and friends.

A WORD FROM THE AUTHOR

The following chapters are insights the Holy Spirit has given me for my personal growth in the Christian walk. They are not meant to be taken verbatim but to be used as a guide for righteous living.

Throughout this book there is a continual reference by the Lord to judging. This does not pertain to judging that is led by the Holy Spirit. The Lord cautions us however, to be sure it is the Holy Spirit leading and not our flesh.

B & B MINISTRIES
P. O. Box 246
Pauma Valley, CA 92061
(619) 742-2320

AUTHOR BIOGRAPHY

Betty Jorgensen Carr was born and raised in Toronto, Canada. She was the youngest of six and a "change of life" baby. Her mother used to introduce her to her friends as "Betty, my mistake".

Those words, spoken in innocence by her mother, provided the foundation for Betty's view of herself and set up the events in her life. Feeling somehow that she had gotten on this earth by some mistake, she tried to prove that she was really okay. She excelled in school, doing her best in almost everything including athletics.

Her mother often sent Betty up to a little Pentecostal church, while she napped. It was there that Betty, at the age of five, accepted Jesus. She made a covenant with Him, that He could use her in any way He saw fit. She even dreamed of becoming a missionary.

She met her husband Poul at age sixteen, married him at age nineteen. She knew he was not a Christian but felt the Lord would remedy that obstacle. They moved to California where they had two children, Susan Lee and Paul Michael. Both children are happily married and have blessed Betty with three wonderful grandchildren.

No matter what successes she enjoyed, Betty carried with her the fear she really wasn't supposed to be here. This fear became so strong that eventually it ruled her life. She was always trying to make peace in her home, when what was really needed was a strong mother and wife.

Unable to "fix" the many problems that plagued their family, Betty turned to alcohol in order to cope. She was smoking 3 1/2 packs of cigarettes a day, and taking valium along with the alcohol. In desperation, she called out to the Lord for help. God in his mercy delivered her from all her addictions. Betty, however, did not experience an instant healing. She asked God daily to help her overcome alcohol, cigarettes and drugs. At this time, she was going through the change of life and her body went into shock. She was thrown into a pit of despair, a hole so black she felt all alone, Yet, she clung to Jesus and he delivered her.

Betty went back to church and it was there the Lord spoke to her saying, "do not read any books, or listen to any tapes. Just read my bible and I will teach you" In this book, are some of the lessons given her directly from the Holy Spirit. Betty hopes you can learn as she has learned the true march of faith it takes to walk the victorious walk.

The Lord gave Betty a love and the heart necessary to work with the homeless in her area. Her experiences with alcohol, drugs and that terrible black pit of depression, have enabled her to successfully share God with many of the homeless.

She has counselled men and women who have been molested and abused both verbally and physically, those with rejection and low self-esteem, and drug addicts. She has also been sent on missions for the Lord to Jerusalem and Canada and is looking forward to traveling for him further.

She had been in charge of her church's feeding of the homeless for ten years. Seeing a need that was not being met, she founded Operation Warm-Up, with a goal that it would eventually go nationwide. During the last six years, through the efforts of Operation Warm-Up, thousands of sleeping bags, blankets, tarps, and socks have been unconditionally given to disaster victims, the elderly, children and the less fortunate.

The Lord had delivered Betty from the fear that had ruled her life, along with rejection and low self-esteem; however because she refused to abandon Jesus, Betty's 38 year marriage did not survive. Her husband left her for another woman.

Rejected, alone, feeling abandoned and a failure, the Lord sustained her. She is a living example of Galatians 2:20: **"I have been crucified with Christ and I no longer live, but Christ lives in me. The life I live in the body, I live by faith in the Son of God, who love me and gave himself for me."**

It has been five years since Poul left Betty, a time of healing, renewal and faith followed.

Today Betty lives in a quiet community with her new husband William Carr. Bill, a minister also, stands alongside Betty as her covering and partner in God's work. As they travel, Betty shares God's word as she teaches and lectures.

She is living proof that God can and will uphold you, even in your darkest hour. We pray this book will encourage you and help you along the victorious path to spiritual fulfillment.

Lecturer, author, prophet, ordained minister, teacher, Reverend Carr comes to life when she is sharing the Lord.

Betty's prayer is for you to read this book and discover how walking and living the Christian life is not complicated. One must have a willing, dedicated and loving heart towards Jesus Christ our Savior. The Holy Spirit is indeed a person, it's Betty's best friend, teacher, and comforter.

> "Living a Christian life takes a life time of effort,
>   and yet the Holy Spirit speaks to us in a simple
>   and uncomplicated manner," says Betty.
> "The Holy Spirit tells us how to deal with the
>   many problems we face along with how to let
>   the old nature die; it gives us further insights
>   into Christian living. The Holy Spirit truly
>   desires to commune with us, it will not
>   leave us weaponless."

The following chapters are insights the Holy Spirit has given Betty on walking the Christian life. She is still in the middle of learning, but constantly falling and being picked up in the loving arms of the Holy Spirit. She prays each reader will be blessed with these simple, yet profound lessons.

> *"If anyone chooses to do God's will,*
> *he will find out whether my teaching comes*
> *from God or whether I speak on my own."*
> *(John 7:17, NIV)*

SECTION ONE
HOW WE HANDLE THE
PROBLEMS WE FACE

Chapter One

ANXIETY AND ANGUISH

"My people, what would you have me do? Have I not given you my son? Has He not died for your sins? Have I not given you love and guidance? I would ask, nay demand loyalty.

"When you entertain doubts, fears, anxieties, do you not see that you are not only listening to Satan but doing his work for him? Where is the witness when you doubt? Yet there can be glory when you say "in God I trust, He will look after me, my needs". Not only say it, but mean it and feel it to your very depths. When an anxious thought comes into your mind and you entertain it, where is the glory to me? It is a victory for Satan."

> *"For our struggle is not against flesh and blood,*
> *but against the rulers, against the authorities, against*
> *he powers of this dark world and against the spiritual*
> *forces of evil in the heavenly realms." (Ephesians 6:12, NIV)*

"To live the victorious life, you must accept in your very depths, my love, my caring, my guidance. You must know in your depths, I will not let you fall. You must trust me, every part of you. Then and only then can you walk with true freedom. True freedom comes from shaking off doubts, anxieties - true freedom comes from my word."

"Cast all your anxiety on him because he cares for you. Be self-controlled and alert. Your enemy the devil prowls around like a roaring lion looking for someone to devour. Resist him, standing firm in the faith, because you know that your brothers throughout the world are undergoing the same kind of sufferings. And the God of all grace, who called you to his eternal glory in Christ, after you have suffered a little while, will himself restore you and make you strong, firm and steadfast. To him be the power for ever and ever. Amen." (1 Peter 5:7-11, NIV)

"This is not to say you need no longer pray to be upheld. You are to pray for each other and uphold each other for this is indeed a battle we are in. There are constant battles going on. When you smile, and say, "praise the Lord" when any kind of adversity comes, it is a victory for me which in turn is a victory for you, for it strengthens your faith and strengthens your resolve."

"Be on your guard; stand firm in the faith; be men of courage; be strong." (1 Corinthians 16:13, NIV)

"Do not underestimate your opponent for he goes about seeking who he can devour. He would like to see you fail! Satan is so full of hate that he is utterly merciless."

"Be sober, be vigilant; because your adversary the devil, as a roaring lion, walketh about, seeking whom he may devour:" (1 Peter 5:8, NIV)

"I would have you all learn the victorious walk. Count it all joy and you have the secret, the secret to defeating failure, which gives me the victory which strengthens your faith and resolve."

"The Lord is my strength and my shield; my heart trusts in him, and I am helped. My heart leaps for joy and I will give thanks to him in song." (Psalms 28:7, NIV)

"Stand in faith and receive this word for it is not to be taken lightly.

"Anguish is not of me. It is and has been Satan's effective tool. Anguish is a large part of our flesh. For example: you hurt someone by speaking harshly to them; or they were unkind to you, even more, cruel to you and rather than turning to me, you anguish over it.

"Check with me to see if there is any truth to any criticism you have received. Repent and ask forgiveness if you have inadvertently hurt someone. No one wants to think they have done harm. Yet, through these revelations come healing, insight and an awareness of our character defects. As in any defect, it must be straightened out before we can go on. It is so with my revelations of your life. Some are painful revelations of when you were children, yet, with my guidance, that area can and will be healed."

"Then your light will break forth like the dawn, and your healing will quickly appear; then your right - eousness will go before you, and the glory of the LORD will be your rear guard." (Isaiah 58:8, NIV)

"Anguish is also part of ego (pride). Know and feel the truth of this. Also be aware that I see the heart. When you repent, truly repent then, know and rest in the knowledge of your forgiveness. If you allow anguish in, you beat yourselves unmercifully."

"When pride comes, then comes disgrace, but with humility comes wisdom." (Proverbs 11:2, NIV)

"Know I love each and everyone of you for your humanity. It gives me great pleasure to set you free. It brings joy to my angels and there is rejoicing in heaven when a person accepts Jesus Christ as their Savior, and is set free. Know and understand, that if this is a war, as I have said it is, does it not stand to reason that the angels in heaven rejoice with each freeing? As the freeing of accepting me occurs, you not only are drawn closer to me, but you can hear me more clearly."

> *"In my anguish I cried to the LORD, and he answered by setting me free."* **(Psalms 118:5, NIV)**

"Realize children that (1) anguish is not of me, (2) revelations are meant to be freeing and healing, therefore there should be rejoicing and praising of me, and (3) take care not to heap condemnation on yourselves for condemnation is not of me."

> *"Therefore, there is now no condemnation for those who are in Christ Jesus."* **(Romans 8:1, NIV)**

"Know children, that I guide and direct. Satan does not like to see anyone set free and therefore takes perverse pleasure in trying to stop it. When this is realized, you have a tool. Tell Satan his lies can not hold water. Tell him that his lies have been brought to the surface and you won't listen to them any more."

> *"But for you who revere my name, the sun of right - eousness will rise with healing in its wings. And you will go out and leap like calves released from the stall."* **(Malachi 4:2, NIV)**

"Stand on the defenses I have given you. My word, which is your sword. My blood which is your weapon. And faith which is your tool. Satan cannot stand it when you use these. Know this, hide it in your hearts and you will be victorious. Victorious against Satan's lies. This is a march of victory that everyone is in, and I guide you."

> *"The weapons we fight with are not the weapons of the world. On the contrary, they have divine power to demolish strongholds."* **(2 Corinthians 10:4, NIV)**

"The troubles of my heart have multiplied; free me from my anguish." (Psalms 25:17, NIV)

"I will be glad and rejoice in your love, for you saw my affliction and knew the anguish of my soul." (Psalms 31:7, NIV)

A.   LOW SELF–ESTEEM

"Anxious thoughts are destroyers of faith and trust. They back up the lie of unworthiness and low self–esteem. They are not only the door to the evil one, but most of the key. Anxious thoughts can be in the form of persecution (unreasoning dislike or suspicion). They can open the door to anger, fears, low self–esteem and can open you up to pride. That person doesn't know as much as me, or look at what they're doing, I would never do that. It can open the door to most of Satan's strong men (evil spirits). If you learn to always check with me, you will be able to detect if you have done something wrong. Then you can rest in the knowledge you will be forgiven so no anxious thought can enter."

Then I acknowledged my sin to you and did not cover up my iniquity. I said, "I will confess my transgressions to the LORD" —and you forgave the guilt of my sin." (Psalms 32:5, NIV)

"Guilt is the companion of anxious thoughts."

"Put all your trust in me and lean not to your own understanding." (Prov. 3:5-6, NIV)

"You now have a key—a key to victorious living. A key to me. Anxious thoughts, accompanied by guilt, let your flesh take over and block my workings, block my spirit and block my blessings. Ask me for eyes that see and ears that hear and this will all come to life for you. This is another freeing of a bondage, and, coupled with a willing heart, makes you victorious in me. Walk the straight and narrow, feel my love, guidance, support and love along the way."

"You are my refuge and my shield; I have put my hope in your word." (Psalms 119:114, NIV)

B.   MISUNDERSTANDINGS

"At times, some of you are misunderstood, you say one thing when another is meant. Take care not to take offense where none is intended. Check with me when someone criticizes, know I do not heap condemnation. However, I do speak through others sometimes. Have you not been used that way? The key is take no offense when none is meant. If a brother or sister comes to you with an idea you're not sure of or a complaint, say thank you — I'll check with God. **Then do it,** taking care not to take offense when none is meant. Stand firm, do what I say in the above and all will be well."

"Search me, O God, and know my heart; test me and know my anxious thoughts." (Psalms 139:23, NIV)

"It is the same with anxious thoughts. These thoughts come from a lie, either of your flesh or of the evil one. Again, check with me. Anxious thoughts open the door to the evil one, giving him permission to create havoc. See you not? Entertaining or believing an anxious thought says you believe the lie of the enemy. Always check with me. I am faithful and just."

"Do not be anxious about anything, but in everything, by prayer and petition, with thanksgiving, present your requests to God." (Philippians 4:6, NIV)

"I do not give anxious thoughts, know also that I cannot work through anxious thoughts. Such thoughts block or stop the blessings. That is why Satan loves to plague you with them. Be warned however, it is not always Satan but you yourself, your own flesh that produces anxious thoughts. Bring your flesh to the cross every day, bind and bring into captivity any thought exalting itself above me.

Lift all areas of your life to me, and you will find I am
faithful and just. The rewards of following this instruction
are peace and serenity."

*"An anxious heart weighs a man down, but a kind word
cheers him up."* **(Proverbs 12:25, NIV)**

C. TAKING OFFENSE

"By taking offense you open yourself to unforgiveness
and hurt, then it opens the door to misunderstanding. I
would warn you all of the danger of taking offense."

*"Be kind and compassionate to one another, forgiving
each other, just as in Christ God forgave you."*
(Ephesians 4:32, NIV)

"How do you not take offense? Ask me if a remark is
true or not. Search yourself and see whether the criticism is
valid or not. If it is not, do not accept it. Say to yourself, I
do not accept that. Offensive words or actions can be a tool
of the enemy, usually re-enforcing rejection, and worth-
lessness. They also try to bring in unforgiveness and bitterness. If the remark is true, learn from it and rectify any
wrong that you can. Criticism can be good if it is truly con-
structive."

*"For I see that you are full of bitterness and captive to
sin."* **(Acts 8:23, NIV)**

"As you learn to walk closer to me, the enemy will use
subtle tools to try to destroy your confidence. A return to
the old habit of fear and anxiety are such tools. They also
allow in self-pity." Criticism can be good if it is con-
structive, however remember:

*"Therefore, there is now no condemnation for those who
are in Christ Jesus."* **(Romans 8:1, NIV)**

"Being quick to take offense is one of Satan's weapons not often discussed. It requires you to take your eyes off me and focus on yourself or certain circumstances. It leads to walls of separation being built around you, causing hurt and a sense of isolation. It sometimes makes people seem unapproachable.

"Can you now see the danger in being quick to take offense? It also opens the door to misunderstanding. You are to check with me to see whether a criticism is correct or not. If it is not, ask for insight into the person giving the criticism. Perhaps there is deep hurt in their life, jealousy or just simple misunderstanding. Pray for them. It says in my word to love those who seem unlovable. Critics or offense makers, may seem unlovable, at least to you."

"We put no stumbling-block in anyone's path, so that our ministry will not be discredited." (2 Corinthians 6:3, NIV)

"It is bad to accept offense and hurt. Take care not to give it! People can be used by Satan without being aware of it and I bring this to your attention."

"Do not cause anyone to stumble, whether Jews, Greeks or the church of God." (1 Corinthians 10:32, NIV)

"A rule of thumb is, what would Jesus do? He would walk in love, at all times, through all circumstances. Learn the danger of giving offense. Be aware of the spirits to whom you open a door. Be aware, look at the log in your **own** eye."

"Why do you look at the speck of sawdust in your brother's eye and pay no attention to the plank in your own eye?" (Matthew 7:3, NIV)

"Remember Satan's job is not only to steal your joy and your peace, but to destroy you by separating us. Do not allow yourself to be used in this way. If you take offense, you can also go to your brother or sister and ask what they meant. Quite often you misinterpret or misunderstand what is being said or the other person wasn't even aware of the offense. Being open and honest while walking in love will defeat this problem.

"Do not be drawn into a circumstance that hurts someone. Remember, do not relay information about something someone else has said. Do not take sides, do not encourage gossip but rather ask the person if they are sure they understood correctly and if they did, say, 'let's pray for them'. There is not only strength in prayer but great healing and comfort. It is hard to hate someone for whom you pray."

"But now you must rid yourselves of all such things as these: anger, rage, malice, slander and filthy language from your lips." (Colossians 3:8, NIV)

D.   TURNING THINGS OVER TO THE LORD

"Rest and know I am your Lord. Rest and know I shelter you. Yea, though the storms of life are all around you in misunderstanding, confusion, and evil works; rest in the knowledge that I, your Lord God, hold you.

"Remember, examine every thought not based on compassion or love. My way is one of peace, love, understanding and compassion. There have been and will continue to be snares set for you. Keep this uppermost in your minds, yield to me and all will be well. Take care for every time you walk outside my covering, every time you go the evil one's way, every time you make a wrong turn, he is there waiting to steal your blessing."

"Finally, be strong in the Lord and in his mighty power." (Ephesians 6:10, NIV)

"I say to you, joy, peace and contentment are really not that hard to gain, especially for those with a great love of me. The way is to leave your old self and become a total new person in Christ Jesus. Yield to me your new nature and, in so doing, defeat of the enemy and your life will be complete."

"We live by faith, not by sight." (2 Corinthians 5:7, NIV)

"Not that you won't go through these trials or perhaps even worse, but you can go through them with a song in your heart and praises on your lips - hence defeating your enemy once and for all in your life. Do not forget anxiety is a tool of Satan's and unless you have turned all to me, how can you help but experience anxiety and, in so doing, allow torment inside your mind and heart."

"I always thank my God as I remember you in my prayers." (Philemon 1:4, NIV)

"Take this to heart for in it is your key, your key to living an anxiety free life, even in the midst of stormy turmoil. Know this then, make it your goal in all things, finances, work, and in everything you do or that is done to you."

"Therefore put on the full armor of God, so that when the day of evil comes, you may be able to stand your ground, and after you have done everything, to stand." (Ephesians 6:13, NIV)

"Satan can use your family or loved ones mightily but never forget greater is He who is in you then he who is of this world. You do fight principalities of darkness and unless you safely yield to me, your Lord God, how could you help but be buffeted by the storms of life."

"For our struggle is not against flesh and blood, but against the rulers, against the authorities, against the powers of this dark world and against the spiritual forces of evil in the heavenly realms." (Ephesians 6:12, NIV)

"Take that step in faith by laying down any and all anxious thoughts at my altar and leaving them; ask and inwardly invite my peace and keep it; rebuke, bind and cast out any fear, anxiety or pride in the name of Jesus."

"You are my refuge and my shield; I have put my hope in your word." **(Psalms 119:114, NIV)**

"This is a key, a key to an anxiety free life. Use it, and peace will be yours."

"Who of you by worrying can add a single hour to his life?" **(Matthew 6:27, NIV)**

"Do not let any unwholesome talk come out of your mouths, but only what is helpful for building others up according to their needs, that it may benefit those who listen." **(Ephesians 4:29, NIV)**

Chapter Two

FOLLOWING MY WORD

A. EVANGELIZING

"Some of you have different paths, each is unique, each has his gifts, talents. You are all where you are for a purpose. All part of the body, doing my will.

"Most of you would be totally lost if you were in each other's shoes. What is hard for one, is easy for another. Hence, some of you can fellowship only with Christians and that is an important thing, for it is a responsibility to uphold each other, laugh with them, bless them... that's what fellowship is all about."

"It was he who gave some to be apostles, some to be prophets, some to be evangelists, and some to be pastors and teachers." (Ephesians 4:11, NIV)

"All are called to evangelize, yet there are some of you called to be evangelists. To let your light shine to the darkened world, the path and road is made easy because I have paved the way. The path is easy, because I have prepared the hearts. The path is also a lonely path but rewarding. Be strong against temptation."

*"In the same way, let your light shine before men, that
they may see your good deeds and praise your Father
in heaven." (Matthew 5:16, NIV)*

"Know I love you all equally. No one is more loved then
another. Without the evangelist, where would you be, where
would the lost souls be? Without fellowship and talking
about me, where would our church be? "Prayer warriors are
as needed as evangelists, no one more then another."

"Pray continually." (1 Thessalonians 5:17, NIV)

"Suffice it to say, your roles were laid out before you
were born. Your uniqueness was from me. It is only the
world's shackles that have to come off. Know this, I see
each of you as my beautiful creations with pure hearts."

*"But if we walk in the light, as he is in the light, we
have fellowship with one another, and the blood of
Jesus, his Son, purifies us from all sin." (1 John 1:7, NIV)*

"As each freeing comes, you become more and more like
me, which is the you I made. Rest easy children, you are all
being used. Make sure, you submit your will to me, then all
will be well."

Additional references: **1 Corinthians 12; Ephesians 4:16**

B.   A PURE AND WILLING HEART

"A pure and willing heart is when you love me above all
others. When you turn to me first in time of despair and
when you learn the fear of the Lord."

*"Teach me your way, O LORD, and I will walk in your
truth; give me an undivided heart, that I may fear your
name." (Psalms 86:11, NIV)*

"A pure and willing heart would rather die then displease
me. A pure and willing heart does everything to please me;
not for rewards, but because it loves me above all else."

"If you are willing and obedient, you will eat the best from the land." (Isaiah 1:19, NIV)

"A pure and willing heart is a giving heart, a generous heart that seeks only to do my will. A pure and willing heart is obedient to my commands, will not tolerate any obstacle in its path to do my will. Most, but not all pure and willing hearts have been delivered from the hands of Satan, so they know and feel in their very depths, my goodness."

"He lifted me out of the slimy pit, out of the mud and mire; he set my feet on a rock and gave me a firm place to stand." (Psalms 40:2, NIV) "I desire to do your will, O my God; your law is within my heart." (Psalms 40:8, NIV)

"Anyone can have a pure and willing heart. It takes dedication to my will, dedication to me in all things. It asks your all but the rewards far outweigh what you give."

"Blessed are the pure in heart, for they will see God." (Matthew 5:8, NIV)

"The first prerequisite is wanting my will and my will alone. It calls for a dedication to me that a lot are afraid of or are not willing to give. Weigh this carefully for a pure and willing heart carries a responsibility also. If you feel you would like a pure and willing heart, then do as the song says and surrender all. If it seems too hard for you, know that I love you and will sustain you.

"All are not generals, all are not sergeants, all do not have pure and willing hearts. Do not allow condemnation upon yourselves for I love you all. This is meant for an understanding. Know I love you all equally. Know you are all my sons and daughters and know when you falter, I will be there."

"Finally, be strong in the Lord and in his mighty power." (Ephesians 6:10, NIV)

C. ENVY

"Know and feel in your hearts, that envy is not of me. Part of the secret of dealing with envy is knowing where you stand with me. If you have your eyes on me alone, how can envy come in? When you are in my service, doing my will, how can envy come in?

"Envy is an abhorrent sin, a twin to jealousy. They are not only devastating, they are killers. Killers of your self-esteem, killers of your feelings of self-worth. It is also a sin that can cause breaks in relationship faster then any other. Envy and jealousy are of the evil one. If you are aware that envy and jealousy have been a very successful tactic of Satan in the past, perhaps you can understand it today."

> *"For where you have envy and selfish ambition, there you find disorder and every evil practice."*
> *(James 3:16, NIV)*

"Envy can be combatted by walking in my ways, praising me and worshipping me. Know you not, I am everything that envy and jealousy is not? Where there is love, how can there be jealousy? Know children and feel my love. If you love and are loved, you'll want to share and not hoard love.

"Ask for a generous heart, ask for a loving heart. Do you not see? Therein lies the victory over envy and jealousy."

> *"And this is my prayer: that your love may abound more and more in knowledge and depth of insight, so that you may be able to discern what is best and may be pure and blameless until the day of Christ, filled with the fruit of righteousness that comes through Jesus Christ—to the glory and praise of God."*
> *(Philippians 1:9-11, NIV)*

"Rebuke and bring to light any lies the enemy may put upon your heart. Example: she hears from God, why don't I? or she's so bossy, she hurts my feelings, who does she think she is? The solution? Pray for them. Ask me to touch anyone's life toward whom you feel even the slightest twinge of jealousy. This brings about restoration, peace and love in the relationship. Lastly, know I am always beside each of you, if I am for you, who is against you?"

> *"What, then, shall we say in response to this? If God is for us, who can be against us?"* **(Romans 8:31, NIV)**

"Ask my forgiveness and rest in the knowledge that you are forgiven when you feel envy and repent. Am I not merciful and just?"

> *"If we confess our sins, he is faithful and just and will forgive us our sins and purify us from all unright - eousness."* **(1 John 1:9, NIV)**

"Practice this children and you will be victorious. This too, is another way of breaking a bondage."

D.   INTOLERANCE

"Tolerance is something most people think they have until a situation comes into their lives to show them otherwise. For example: I have waited so long I'm getting tired of waiting... anger and intolerance comes from others making you wait.

"Intolerance is a subtle tool of the enemy, used most effectively. It starts with simple things such as being overlooked in line, to intolerance of other's religious beliefs."

> *"If anyone considers himself religious and yet does not keep a tight rein on his tongue, he deceives himself and his religion is worthless."* **(James 1:26, NIV)**

"Intolerance is subtle and, unless you are aware of its tactics, it can fester and grow. Intolerance when allowed to run rampant, leads to bondage to Satan, and it can produce men such as Hitler, Stalin, and Ku Klux Klan members."

"For out of the heart come evil thoughts, murder,
adultery, sexual immorality, theft, false testimony,
slander." (Matthew 15:19, NIV)

"Intolerance can get a foothold with such subtlety, thus making it a deadly enemy of every Christian. Too often, intolerance is tolerated for the sake of peace, but I say to you, unless it is routed out, how can you have peace?

"When you have a friend, a neighbor, a loved one, showing any intolerance, we should show reproof of such attitude. For instance, if you hear someone say "my gosh, she's dumb"... that's not only judgmental but a statement of intolerance. The Christian way is... how can I help her gain confidence, how can I help her with an obvious problem she has? Do you see the difference?"

"For man's anger does not bring about the righteous
life that God desires." (James 1:20, NIV)

"When you hear someone say she's not born again, or she's in a cult, rather than an intolerant viewpoint, you should say... does my demeanor show the Lord's love. Can I bring the truth to them without turning them off? There is a fine line here, and one that must always be broached with a non-judgmental attitude.

"Can you see how the enemy has used intolerance for years and how it grows and opens the door to anger, bigotry, pride, judgmental religiosity? Intolerance should be fought against as hard as you fight bigotry, for intolerance is bigotry's root. Pride has its root in intolerance; anger has its root in intolerance. Every wicked thought has intolerance connected to it."

"Get rid of all bitterness, rage and anger, brawling and
slander, along with every form of malice."
(Ephesians 4:31, NIV)

"Bind the spirits of intolerance. Be aware and on guard of it. It can come in under the guise of justification, such as, I deserve that, or I worked hard for it.

"Do you not see? The enormity of intolerance cannot be stressed enough. Be warned. Be on guard and be ever vigilant. Of what act of intolerance are you guilty?

"Intolerance is so against my nature. On judgment day, when people say, but Jesus, we knew you, we were mighty tools for you, I will say to them... I knew you not, for it was in my name you hurt someone, it was in my name you made them outcasts, in my name you had them turn from me because of your intolerance, because of your bigotry. I shall spew you out of my mouth."

> *"They also will answer, Lord, when did we see you hungry or thirsty or a stranger or needing clothes or sick or in prison, and did not help you?"*
> *(Matthew 25:44, NIV)*

"Be on guard against intolerance. Watch for it in your churches. If you give it a foothold, it will take hold, fester and your church will die. My word and my word alone is solid rock. All else is sinking ground."

> *"Your attitude should be the same as that of Christ Jesus."* *(Philippians 2:5, NIV)*

"Stand on my word, walk in my love and intolerance cannot get a foothold. This insight is given you, so you can do battle. Do not allow intolerance to get a foothold. Hold fast to my truth for the end is near; for the chaff is being sifted from the wheat. Hold fast for the rewards are mighty and beyond your imagination.

"Wait for me, love one another, be at peace for the end is near, so says your Lord God.

"Intolerance is such an enemy, you must understand it better. Knowing your enemy well, gives you the advantage. You will have the advantage over the tactics of the enemy. You will have the advantage of knowing the enemy works subtly and not so subtly. Intolerance is to be fought as hard as you fight anything else, for intolerance is at the base of almost all defaming acts, almost all evil thoughts.

"Intolerance can fill people with what they think is righteous indignation, when in reality it is religiosity. When you feel righteously indignant, check your motive out, check with me, check my word."

"But for those who are self-seeking and who reject the truth and follow evil, there will be wrath and anger." *(Romans 2:8, NIV)*

"So much heartache and destructions have come about under the guise of righteous indignation, when in reality it is intolerance. Do you now see the enormity of this? Intolerance comes in other ways. Intolerance of another person's color. Example: Blacks are alright, but not like us; or Catholics are all right, but not born again. I say to you, beware of this, be always on guard."

"Religion that God our Father accepts as pure and faultless is this: to look after orphans and widows in their distress and to keep oneself from being polluted by the world." *(James 1:27, NIV)*

"Intolerance can come so hidden, that before you know it, it can become full blown and spread its disease. Unless it is cut out at the root, it will return and return. You can be intolerant of someone's gifts, looking at them with suspicion because their gift is different from yours. Intolerance can only come when you put your understanding above mine, when you construct those walls, so you won't get hurt or be made to feel inadequate. You are being intolerant when you do this, for you have pre-judged another's motives.

Example: (1) They cannot be trusted or (2) they can hurt you, so you put walls up that no one can break through. Remember, your walls even shut me out. This is judgmental, even if you think it is only protecting yourself."

"Have you not discriminated among yourselves and become judges with evil thoughts?" *(James 2:4, NIV)*

"Do you not see the devious way intolerance gets its tentacles into you? In our churches, we are encouraged to open ourselves up and truly love a stranger, yet some feel it is a risk. They also feel it is a risk to give another as much leeway as you yourself desire, and a risk to appreciate, uphold and love one another and a risk to be thankful you are all different.

"Do you not see? If you are not willing to take a risk, if you are not willing to trust, if you are not willing to ask for help, if you are not willing to enjoy someone else's gifts and to praise me and appreciate them, intolerance can come into your heart."

"Search me, O God, and know my heart; test me and know my anxious thoughts." (Psalms 139:23, NIV)

"When you are in battle for me, when you are in the front lines for me, these are things for which you must look out."

"I want men everywhere to lift up holy hands in prayer, without anger or disputing." (1 Timothy 2:8, NIV)

"Suffice it to say, be ever vigilant and on guard against intolerance. Stand by one another, for that is the will of Christ Jesus, your Savior."

"As it is, there are many parts, but one body. The eye cannot say to the hand, "I don't need you!" And the head cannot say to the feet, "I don't need you!" (1 Corinthians 12:20-21, NIV)

NOTE; Throughout this book there is a continual reference by the Lord to judging. This does not pertain to judgment that is led by the **Holy Spirit.** The Lord cautions us however, to be sure it **is** the Holy Spirit leading and not our flesh.

Chapter Three

STEWARDSHIP

A. MONEY AND OVERSPENDING GUIDELINES

"It is I who have given you all you have. You must remember, I am a loving Father and, as such, I love to give you gifts as long as it does not corrupt you. Also know I allow you to have money, to see what you will do with it. Many people go on spending binges, many people spend it unwisely yet, most of all, people fail to **ask** me if or how they should spend it."

"No one can serve two masters. Either he will hate the one and love the other, or he will be devoted to the one and despise the other. You cannot serve both God and Money." (Matthew 6:24, NIV)

"Therefore I tell you, do not worry about your life, what you will eat or drink; or about your body, what you will wear. Is not life more important than food, and the body more important than clothes? Look at the birds of the air; they do not sow or reap or store away in barns, and yet your heavenly Father feeds them. Are you not much more valuable than they?"
(Matthew 6:25-26, NIV)

CHECK YOURSELF

(1) "**Motive:** If you desire something, ask yourself why you want it. Do you want it to impress someone? Or make yourself feel good? Ask yourself if its necessary, or how much will it be used?

(2) ·**Purpose:** Will it further my kingdom? Will it bring glory to my name?

"Practice this even with minor things and everything will fall into place. The wealth of the world is gone in a flash, but the most precious gifts are your life and your free will. Beware of excess. That is the spark for overspending. Know what is important to your life and what is not. Battle over-indulgence. What does anything matter if your soul is lost? What does anything matter if you spend eternity away from me? Oh, don't you see, what is important and what is not? Keep your priorities straight and all will be well.

"You must remember, everyone lives within a circle of friends. Usually if you live with medium to low income it is easier to handle your money, for you must budget. However, it is a difficult path for the Christian that has much. They have the temptation of buying to please them-selves, they have the temptation to "play God", because they see other people's needs, and have the money to rectify their situation. It is very important to ask me if you should help a particular person. It is good to have a generous heart with money, however, that can lead to unwise spending, much to your own detriment."

"For the love of money is a root of all kinds of evil. Some people, eager for money, have wandered from the faith and pierced themselves with many griefs."
(1 Timothy 6:10, NIV)

"So when you give to the needy, do not announce it with trumpets, as the hypocrites do in the synagogues and on the streets, to be honored by men. I tell you the truth, they have received their reward in full. But when you give to the needy, do not let your left hand know what your right hand is doing." (Matthew 6:2-3, NIV)

"Many people have done this and found themselves in debt. They moan and groan and blame it on everything, except themselves. Did they ask me to guide them? Did they help another to their own detriment, without asking me? Once they are in a predicament of being in debt, due to their own error, they must ask me where they went wrong, tighten their belt to get out of debt, asking me to help them and give them another chance.

"Keep your lives free from the love of money and be content with what you have, because God has said," *"Never will I leave you; never will I forsake you." (Hebrews 13:5, NIV)*

"To wait, brings blessings. When you overspend, do not allow yourself to get so filled with remorse that you pour condemnation on yourself. Just learn from it. Do not be impulsive. If you can learn to harness your enthusiasm, it can and will be used for my glory.

"Take care for the evil one would have you so overwhelmed with debt, and then so filled with remorse and despair, that it leads to worry, and worry stops me from working in your life.

"Again, I reiterate, check with me, check your motive. Ask if it would bring me glory or you glory. There are many trials in life, many tests to overcome. Some of you see yourselves as failures, as phony, fearing if someone who got to know you, they wouldn't like you. So, some hide in alcohol or in overeating to prove they are really not lovable, then indulge in over spending on material things, to prove they are worth something. You see, you live in a world of conflicting messages, one fighting the other.

"How do you get off this merry-go-round? (1) Know you are lovable. (2) Know your worth. (3) Lay all your troubles and cares at my feet. (4) Ask me to help you have a speedy recovery in this area of your life.

"I say to you, it is up to you whether you will listen to the lies of the enemy, or to come with me through the door to freedom.

"Your self-worth does not depend on appearance. It does not depend on people. It depends wholly on your relationship with me and I say to you, I will set you free. You have allowed circumstances to come and torment you because you do not realize how I value you.

"This is a time to get right before me and know I love you. If you can concentrate on that, then when it comes to spending you can ask me. All is up to you, but woe to you who are left on your own. Those desiring my will, willing to do my will, will receive my help. So says the Lord."

> *"And why do you worry about clothes? See how the lilies of the field grow. They do not labor or spin. Yet I tell you that not even Solomon in all his splendor was dressed like one of these. If that is how God clothes the grass of the field, which is here today and tomorrow is thrown into the fire, will he not much more clothe you, O you of little faith?"*
> *(Matthew 6:28-30, NIV)*

> *"Whoever loves money never has money enough; whoever loves wealth is never satisfied with his income. This too is meaningless." (Ecclesiastes 5:10, NIV)*

> *"On the first day of every week, each one of you should set aside a sum of money in keeping with his income, saving it up, so that when I come no collections will have to be made." (1 Corinthians 16:2, NIV)*

> *"Do not store up for yourselves treasures on earth, where moth and rust destroy, and where thieves break in and steal. But store heaven, where moth and rust do not destroy, and where thieves do not break in and steal." (Matthew 6:19-20, NIV)*

B.   TITHING

"If you will reverse the law of tithing, (remembering, everything you have is from me) and realize I allow you to keep 90%, it then becomes a joy and not a burden to tithe but 10%."

SECTION TWO

HOW WE TURN THINGS OVER TO GOD

Chapter Four

KNOW YOUR GOD'S CHARACTER

"When circumstances or things of this earth overwhelm you or intrude on your thoughts or your work with me, say Lord, 'I turn this over to you. I pray that you keep my mind open only to you and close my mind or thoughts to the adverse circumstances.' Then praise me for therein is a freeing, beyond comprehension. In order to attain this, you **must** know my character.

A. WHAT I AM
   (1)   LOVE

> "*My command is this: Love each other as I have loved you. Greater love has no-one than this, that he lay down his life for his friends. You are my friends if you do what I command.*" (**John 15:12-14, NIV**)

> "*No, the Father himself loves you because you have loved me and have believed that I came from God.*" (**John 16:27, NIV**)

(2)   FAITHFUL

"Because of the LORD's great love we are not consumed, for his compassion never fail.   They are new every morning; great is your faithfulness." **(Lamentations 3:22-23, NIV)**

*"Let us hold unswervingly to the hope we profess, for he who promised is faithful." **(Hebrews 10:23, NIV)***

(3)   MERCIFUL

*"And he passed in front of Moses, proclaiming, "The LORD, the LORD, the compassionate and gracious God, slow to anger, abounding in love and faithfulness, maintaining love to thousands, and forgiving wickedness, rebellion and sin. Yet he does not leave the guilty unpunished; he punishes the children and their children for the sin of the fathers to the third and fourth generation." **(Exodus 34:6-7, NIV)***

(4)   JUST

*"If we confess our sins, he is faithful and just and will forgive us our sins and purify us from all unright - eousness." **(1 John 1:9, NIV)***

(5) FORGIVING

*"You forgave the iniquity of your people and covered all their sins." **(Psalms 85:2, NIV)***

*"Blessed is he whose transgressions are forgiven, whose sins are covered. Blessed is the man whose sin the LORD does not count against him and in whose spirit is no deceit." **(Psalms 32:1-2, NIV)***

*"If we confess our sins, he is faithful and just and will forgive us our sins and purify us from all unrighteousness." **(1 John 1:9, NIV)***

(6) KIND

"I will not leave you as orphans; I will come to you."
(John 14:18, NIV)

"Your word, O LORD, is eternal; it stands firm in the heavens. Your faithfulness continues through all gen - erations; you established the earth, and it endures."
(Psalms 119:89-90, NIV)

(7) TOLERANT

"Even to your old age and grey hairs I am he, I am he who will sustain you. I have made you and I will carry you; I will sustain you and I will rescue you."
(Isaiah 46:4, NIV)

(8) COMFORTING

"Praise be to the God and Father of our Lord Jesus Christ, the Father of compassion and the God of all comfort, who comforts us in all our troubles, so that we can comfort those in any trouble with the comfort we ourselves have received from God."
(2 Corinthians 1:3-4, NIV)

"As a mother comforts her child, so will I comfort you; and you will be comforted over Jerusalem."
(Isaiah 66:13, NIV)

(9) TRUTH

"Guide me in your truth and teach me, for you are God my Saviour, and my hope is in you all day long."
(Psalms 25:5, NIV)

"Into your hands I commit my spirit; redeem me, O LORD, the God of truth." (Psalms 31:5, NIV)

(10) PEACE

"I have told you these things, so that in me you may have peace. In this world you will have trouble. But take heart! I have overcome the world." (John 16:33, NIV)

(11) TRUSTWORTHY

"Trust in the LORD with all your heart and lean not on your own understanding; in all your ways acknowledge him, and he will make your paths straight." (Proverbs 3:5-6, NIV)

(12) HUMBLE, MEEK, GENTLE

"Take my yoke upon you and learn from me, for I am gentle and humble in heart, and you will find rest for your souls." (Matthew 11:29, NIV)

B. WHAT I, YOUR GOD WILL NOT TOLERATE
(1) OTHER IDOLS

"You have made your bed on a high and lofty hill; there you went up to offer your sacrifices. Behind your doors and your doorpost you have put your pagan symbols. Forsaking me, you uncovered your bed, you climbed into it and opened it wide; you made a pact with those whose beds you love, and you looked on their nakedness." (Isaiah 57:7-8, NIV)

"There is no peace," says my God, "for the wicked." (Isaiah 57:21, NIV)

"For this ye know, that no whoremonger, nor unclean person, nor covetous man, who is an idolater, hath any inheritance in the kingdom of Christ and of God." (Ephesians 5:5, NIV)

(2) GOSSIP

"Get rid of all bitterness, rage and anger, brawling and slander, along with every form of malice. Be kind and compassionate to one another, forgiving each other, just as in Christ God forgave you."
(Ephesians 4:31-32, NIV)

(3) DISOBEDIENCE

*"They claim to know God, but by their actions they deny him. They are detestable, disobedient and unfit for doing anything good." **(Titus 1:16, NIV)***

*"For the eyes of the Lord are on the righteous and his ears are attentive to their prayer, but the face of the Lord is against those who do evil." **(1 Peter 3:12, NIV)***

(4) PERVERSE SEX

*"For whoremongers, for them that defile themselves with mankind, for men-stealers, for liars, for perjured persons, and if there be any other thing that is contrary to sound doctrine; According to the glorious gospel of the blessed God, which was committed to my trust." **(1 Timothy 1:10-11, NIV)***

"Do you not know that the wicked will not inherit the kingdom of God? Do not be deceived: Neither the sexually immoral nor idolaters nor adulterers nor male prostitutes nor homosexual offenders nor thieves nor the greedy nor drunkards nor slanderers nor swindlers will inherit the kingdom of God."
(1 Corinthians 6:9-10, NIV)

(5) PRIDE

*"The LORD detests all the proud of heart. Be sure of this: They will not go unpunished." **(Proverbs 16:5, NIV)***

C. HOW I WISH YOU TO LIVE

(1) FOLLOW THE TEN COMMANDMENTS

"Whoever has my commands and obeys them, he is the one who loves me. He who loves me will be loved by my Father, and I too will love him and show myself to him." (John 14:21, NIV) (Exodus 20:1-17, NIV)

(2) YOU ARE TO LOVE ONE ANOTHER

"A new command I give you: Love one another. As I have loved you, so you must love one another." (John 13:34, NIV)

(3) LIVE IN PEACE AND HARMONY

"The fruit of righteousness will be peace; the effect of righteousness will be quietness and confidence for ever." (Isaiah 32:17, NIV)

"All your sons will be taught by the LORD, and great will be your children's peace." (Isaiah 54:13, NIV)

"For the kingdom of God is not a matter of eating and drinking, but of righteousness, peace and joy in the Holy Spirit, because anyone who serves Christ in this way is pleasing to God and approved by men. Let us therefore make every effort to do what leads to peace and to mutual edification." (Romans 14:17-19, NIV)

(4) USE JESUS AS YOUR MODEL

"Dear friends, do not be surprised at the painful trial you are suffering, as though something strange were happening to you. But rejoice that you participate in the sufferings of Christ, so that you may be overjoyed when his glory is revealed." (1 Peter 4:12-13, NIV)

"Therefore, since Christ suffered in his body, arm yourselves also with the same attitude, because he who has suffered in his body is done with sin."
(1 Peter 4:1, NIV)

D. WHAT I DESIRE

(1) TO COMMUNICATE WITH YOU

"For prophecy never had its origin in the will of man, but men spoke from God as they were carried along by the Holy Spirit." **(2 Peter 1:21, NIV)**

"Then those who feared the LORD talked with each other, and the LORD listened and heard. A scroll of remembrance was written in his presence concerning those who feared the LORD and honored his name."
(Malachi 3:16, NIV)

(2) TO BLESS YOU

"He tends his flock like a shepherd: He gathers the lambs in his arms and carries them close to his heart; he gently leads those that have young." **(Isaiah 40:11, NIV)**

"No weapon forged against you will prevail, and you will refute every tongue that accuses you. This is the heritage of the servants of the LORD, and this is their vindication from me," declares the LORD."
(Isaiah 54:17, NIV)

"Praise be to the God and Father of our Lord Jesus Christ, who has blessed us in the heavenly realms with every spiritual blessing in Christ." **(Ephesians 1:,3 NIV)**

(3) TO MEET YOUR NEEDS

"For I will pour water on the thirsty land, and streams on the dry ground; I will pour out my Spirit on your offspring, and my blessing on your descendants."
(Isaiah 44:3, NIV)

"In righteousness you will be established: tyranny will be far from you; you will have nothing to fear. Terror will be far removed; it will not come near you." **(Isaiah 54:14, NIV)**

(4) TO FREE YOU

"You are my hiding-place; you will protect me from trouble and surround me with songs of deliverance." **(Psalms 32:7, NIV)**

"Then you will know the truth, and the truth will set you free." **(John 8:32, NIV)**

(5) TO SAVE YOU

"But whoever listens to me will live in safety and be at ease, without fear of harm." **(Proverbs 1:33, NIV)**

"The LORD your God is with you, he is mighty to save. He will take great delight in you, he will quiet you with his love, he will rejoice over you with singing." **(Zephaniah 3:17, NIV)**

"For God so loved the world that he gave his one and only Son, that whoever believes in him shall not perish but have eternal life." **(John 3:16, NIV)**

(6) THAT YOU FEAR ME

"Then those who feared the LORD talked with each other, and the LORD listened and heard. A scroll of remembrance was written in his presence concerning those who feared the LORD and honored his name. "They will be mine," says the LORD Almighty, "in the day when I make up my treasured possession. I will spare them, just as in compassion a man spares his son who serves him." **(Malachi 3:16-17, NIV)**

"I am a friend to all who fear you, to all who follow your precepts." (Psalms 119:63, NIV)

(7) THAT YOU REST IN ME

"There remains, then, a Sabbath-rest for the people of God" (Hebrews 4:9, NIV)

"Come to me, all you who are weary and burdened, and I will give you rest." (Matthew 11:28, NIV)

To fear God is not to be afraid of God, but to have reverence and awe.

(8) THAT YOU TRUST IN ME

"As for God, his way is perfect; the word of the LORD is flawless. He is a shield for all who take refuge in him." (Psalms 18:30, NIV)

(9) THAT YOU ACCEPT MY PROMISE OF JOY

"You will go out in joy and be led forth in peace; the mountains and hills will burst into song before you, and all the trees of the field will clap their hands." (Isaiah 55:12, NIV)

"These I will bring to my holy mountain and give them joy in my house of prayer. Their burnt offerings and sacrifices will be accepted on my altar; for my house will be called a house of prayer for all nations." (Isaiah 56:7, NIV)

"You have made known to me the path of life; you will fill me with joy in your presence, with eternal pleasures at your right hand." (Psalms 16:11, NIV)

(10) THAT YOU ACCEPT MY PROMISE OF PEACE

"All your sons will be taught by the LORD, and great will be your children's peace." (Isaiah 54:13, NIV)

(11) THAT YOU HAVE LIFE EVERLASTING

*"Verily, verily, I say unto you, He that believeth on me hath everlasting life." **(John 6:47, NIV)***

*"For the wages of sin is death, but the gift of God is eternal life in Christ Jesus our Lord." **(Romans 6:23, NIV)***

*"Surely goodness and love will follow me all the days of my life, and I will dwell in the house of the LORD for ever." **(Psalms 23:6, NIV)***

(12) THAT THERE BE NO DISEASE

*"But he was pierced for our transgressions, he was crushed for our iniquities; the punishment that brought us peace was upon him, and by his wounds we are healed." **(Isaiah 53:5, NIV)***

(13) THAT YOU SEEK MY DIRECTION

*"The steps of a [good] man are ordered by the LORD: and he delighteth in his way." **(Psalms 37:23, NIV)***

*"Trust in the LORD with all your heart and lean not on your own understanding; in all your ways acknowledge him, and he will make your paths straight. **(Proverbs 3:5-6, NIV)***

(14) THAT YOU SEEK MY PROTECTION

*"Who through faith are shielded by God's power until the coming of the salvation that is ready to be revealed in the last time." **(1 Peter 1:5 ,NIV)***

*"God is our refuge and strength, an ever-present help in trouble." **(Psalms 46:1, NIV)***

(15) THAT YOU SEEK MY WISDOM

"I will instruct you and teach you in the way you should go; I will counsel you and watch over you."
(Psalms 32:8, NIV)

"If any of you lacks wisdom, he should ask God, who gives generously to all without finding fault, and it will be given to him." **(James 1:5, NIV)**

(16) THAT YOU SEEK MY GUIDANCE

"I will instruct you and teach you in the way you should go; I will counsel you and watch over you."
(Psalms 32:8, NIV)

"In your unfailing love you will lead the people you have redeemed. In your strength you will guide them to your holy dwelling." **(Exodus 15:13, NIV)**

(17) THAT YOU FIND HAPPINESS IN ME

"You have made known to me the path of life; you will fill me with joy in your presence, with eternal pleasures at your right hand." **(Psalms 16:11, NIV)**

Chapter Five

TURN THINGS
OVER TO GOD

"Learn to leave things in my hands, they are not only capable but quite willing. This is not an easy lesson, for many things come into play. You must be willing to lay the flesh down; you must also, exercise your faith and you must trust me. You must also humble yourselves."

"Humble yourselves before the Lord, and he will lift you up." (James 4:10, NIV)

"Humbling yourselves is to prostrate yourself before me. Yielding all sorrows, all care to me, your King. To truly humble yourself, you must fully understand who I am. When you know this to your very depths, humbling yourself before me is as natural as breathing. I am majestic, all powerful, omnipresent, knowing all things yet I am also a loving Father, a kind friend."

"Humble yourselves, therefore, under God's mighty hand, that he may lift you up in due time." (1 Peter 5:6, NIV)

"My ire can be terrible and my love the sweetest. I will not tolerate other idols before me. You have an adversary who stalks as a thief in the night, be on guard.

"Unless you can realize my true nature, how can you truly turn everything over to me and not take it back? How can you rebuke any anxious thoughts and how can your spirit eyes come into focus?

"Learn my character. When you get that into your hearts, you willingly and happily give me all burdens without taking them back. When you truly understand my character, you humble yourself."

> *"Therefore, whoever humbles himself like this child is*
> *the greatest in the kingdom of heaven."*
> *(Matthew 18:4, NIV)*

> *"For whoever exalts himself will be humbled, and*
> *whoever humbles himself will be exalted."*
> *(Matthew 23:12, NIV)*

"Do you not see? I am so powerful, so kind and so loving, how can you help but lay all flesh down? Yet know this, I see the heart. I see the 'you' I created. Praise me, worship me, get to know me by reading my word and you will know I am faithful and just, merciful and true."

> *"You hear, O LORD, the desire of the afflicted; you*
> *encourage them, and you listen to their cry."*
> *(Psalms 10:17, NIV)*

"Trust and faith go hand in hand and they lead you not only closer to me, but my children, the blessings flow from the closer fellowship and camaraderie you have with me. To turn things over to me, you have to abide in me. As your Father, your creator, as the one who disciplines, loves, exhorts, sets free, polishes and refines, do you think you can trust me enough to abide in me?"

> *"Remain in me, and I will remain in you. No branch can*
> *bear fruit by itself; it must remain in the vine. Neither*

*can you bear fruit unless you remain in me. I am the
vine; you are the branches. If a man remains in me and
I in him, he will bear much fruit; apart from me you
can do nothing. If anyone does not remain in me, and
he is like a branch that is thrown away and withers;
such branches are picked up, thrown into the fire and
burned. If you remain in me and my words remain in
you, ask whatever you wish, and it will be given you."*
(John 15:4-7, NIV)

"Abiding in me gives such peace, pleasure and contentment. It will take a special abiding to meet the tasks and
the trials for the end times. Abiding in me will keep your
lamps well lit. Abiding in me, opens your spiritual ears to
hear what I am telling and takes the blinders off your eyes.
Oh little ones, to abide in me is the closest of walks. It is a
place of joy unspeakable where no negative circumstance
can penetrate. It is a spiritual place all believers should try
to achieve."

*"He who dwells in the shelter of the Most High will rest
in the shadow of the Almighty. I will say of the LORD,
'He is my refuge and my fortress, my God, in whom I
trust.'"* **(Psalms 91:1-2, NIV)**

"How can you learn this? By knowing me, knowing my
character. To truly know me, you have to love me. It is all
intertwined. Beware of the chords of doubt, guilt and lukewarmness. These are the chords that strangle that walk,
these are the chords that sow discord, and disbelief. Take
care, ask me to thoroughly search your hearts. In order to
take your own hands off and to stop running here and there
without direction, you have to have knowledge of who I am;
my character." (see pages on Gods' character)

*"Brothers, each man, as responsible to God, should
remain in the situation God called him to."*
(1 Corinthians 7:24, NIV)

"When you realize in your innermost self, that I am a good Father, that I will **never** allow more than you can bear, then perhaps you can start to realize, that not only is there **no risk** in putting things in my hands, but relief."

"He will sit as a refiner and purifier of silver; he will purify the Levites and refine them like gold and silver. Then the LORD will have men who will bring offerings in righteousness." (Malachi 3:3, NIV)

"You see, children, adversity can be used for growing, stretching, and a deepening trust in me. That's what the scripture means."

"Trust in the LORD with all thine heart; and lean not unto thine own understanding. In all thy ways acknowledge him, and he shall direct thy paths." (Proverbs 3:5-6, NIV)

"What sometimes appears to you as adversity, is, in reality, a freeing or a blessing in disguise. Trusting in me, also is reverence and fear of the Lord.

"If you will all practice, asking, 'Lord, what can I learn from this? What would you have me do?' Then rejoice, know I am faithful and just. I will not let you fall.

"Sometimes adversity comes in the way of tests. They hone you, polish you and teach you. If you will get in your minds that (1) I am loving and kind, (2) I am capable and willing, (3) I see the greater plan. (4) I am trustworthy and am faithful.

"Then, know this: I, your Lord God, promise you I will always shoulder your cares and I will not let you fall."

"As for you, the anointing you received from him remains in you, and you do not need anyone to teach you. But as his anointing teaches you about all things and as that anointing is real, not counterfeit—just as it has taught you, remain in him. And now, dear children, continue in him, so that when he appears we

*may be confident and unashamed before him at his
coming." (1 John 2:27-28, NIV)*

"You are all my blessed children. Your open heart to my
teachings is a joy to me. Continue to pray and uphold one
another."

*"I write to you, fathers, because you have known him
who is from the beginning. I write to you, young men,
because you are strong, and the word of God lives in
you, and you have overcome the evil one."
(1 John 2:14, NIV)*

Chapter Six

BY SEEKING, HEARING, AND SEEING, WE CAN TURN THINGS OVER TO GOD

"My Spirit has shown you that by studying my character, and the lessons on how to turn things over to me, you can now learn the method in seeking me through developing Spirit eyes, which is seeing through my eyes, opening your ears to hear my voice."

"Seeking me requires ears opened, a willing heart and a yielded spirit and soul."

"But if from there you seek the Lord your God, you will find him if you look for him with all your heart and with all your soul." (Deuteronomy 4:29, NIV)

"You will seek me and find me when you seek me with all your heart." (Jeremiah 29:13, NIV)

"So I say to you: Ask and it will be given to you; seek and you will find; knock and the door will be opened to you." (Luke 11:9, NIV)

"Open, truly open, your hearts to me. Lift all areas of your life and you will find, I am faithful and just. Seeking me, waiting to hear me is a lesson in fortitude, and patience and leads to tranquility and peace."

You will seek me and find me when you seek me with all your heart. (Jeremiah 29:13, NIV)

"Know this, my hand is upon each and everyone. I do lead and long to guide. Seeking me is often a test and/or a lesson for laying your flesh down, for when you seek me your desires are put to rest and your faith grows as you realize my timing, my will is not only right, but perfect for you, perfect for your circumstances.

"As your spirit eyes come into focus, try to look beyond the circumstance. My hand is always at work on your behalf. I do not let you fall. Lay all problems at my feet, then rejoice, and happily wait for my answer."

"Ask and it will be given to you; seek and you will find; knock and the door will be opened to you."
(Matthew 7:7, NIV)

"I am your Lord God, faithful and true, just and merciful. If I clothe the fields in such majesty, how less you? My beloved children, seeking and waiting for my timing is an act of faith and a laying down of the flesh. I wish to draw you all closer to me. Do not be afraid but come to me willingly for I love you, each and everyone."

My heart says of you, "Seek his face! Your face, LORD, I will seek." (Psalms 27:8, NIV)

"Glory in his holy name; let the hearts of those who seek the LORD rejoice." (Psalms 105:3, NIV)

"Blessed are they who keep his statutes and seek him with all their heart." (Psalms 119:2, NIV)

"Ears that hear and eyes that see—the LORD has made them both." (Proverbs 20:12, NIV)

"Seeking my face can be done in numerous ways. One way few people remember or put much importance in, is by seeing the best in everyone. Too many of my people see a glaring fault or sin and hone in on such, letting Satan totally color their thinking of others. If you seek my face, you can look past the fault or sin and see the good in them, just as I o you. If you look only at the bad, you bring even mored hurt feelings and misunderstandings. Many of my children have been turned away, in churches by Christians, with this judgmental attitude. What if you look to the good and help that person, without judging? You then allow more good to surface and you have shown mercy and compassion. You have seen that person through my eyes, hence you not only see my face, but show my face to that person."

"And if your eye causes you to sin, pluck it out. It is better for you to enter the kingdom of God with one eye than to have two eyes and be thrown into hell." (Mark 9:47, NIV)

"Another way to seek my face is giving to the poor and the needy without discrimination for many are hurt, bruised and bloodied souls. What you do for the least of mine, so you do unto me.

"Seeking my face is also reading my word. The more you know me, the easier you see me. I would have each of you ask for spirit eyes to see. Many of you are blinded with sin, guilt or judgmental attitude, and if that is so, how can you see anything clearly, much less me? I am the healer and I would heal your spirit eyes, so you can perceive my wonders, so you can and will see me in your brothers and sisters and therefore you can show my compassion and love.

"Seeking my face takes prayer. Do not forget the prayers of a righteous man, availeth much. Pray to see me, pray the Holy Spirit directs your path to me. Never forget, I can be seen in many ways, in a flower, in a baby's smile and in love given and received.

"Seeking my face is holding your hand out to a brother or sister when they have a need. Does it not say in my word, '...if one wants your cloak give him two? There are so many hurting children... so many that a kind word or a prayer with them and a loving hug would mean so much.'"

"He who gives to the poor will lack nothing, but he who closes his eyes to them receives many curses."
(Proverbs 28:27, NIV)

"Oh children, my heart is grieved to hear and see so many who call themselves Christians and are no better then the Pharisees and the Sadducees. Many look only to their need, their happiness when all the while, inner happiness is in giving joy to others and showing my love through you, thus showing my face and seeing my face."

"The precepts of the LORD are right, giving joy to the heart. The commands of the LORD are radiant, giving light to the eyes." (Psalms 19:8, NIV)

"Lastly, does it not say in my word to love your enemy? That is indeed seeing people through my eyes. If they hurt you, turn the other cheek. Many people get that confused with being a wimp or a door mat. What in reality is meant is giving them a benefit of the doubt, if they let you down, or trod on your feelings, give them the benefit of the doubt again and again, hence turning the other cheek.

"So you see children, there are many ways to seek my face. If you put into practice all of them, this I promise you... not only will your life change, not only will you bring joy to others, but you will see my face by showing it to others, so says your Lord."

"Look on me and answer, O LORD my God. Give light to my eyes, or I will sleep in death" (Psalms 13:3, NIV)

"He said, If you listen carefully to the voice of the LORD your God and do what is right in his eyes, if

you pay attention to his commands and keep all his decrees, I will not bring on you any of the diseases I brought on the Egyptians, for I am the LORD, who heals you." **(Exodus 15:26, NIV)**

"Search me, O God, and know my heart; test me and know my anxious thoughts. See if there is any offensive way in me, and lead me in the way ever - lasting." **(Psalms 139: 23-24, NIV)**

To hear me, you should:

(1) "Start with the above scripture. This will allow my Spirit to tell you if you are clean before me, or if you have any unforgiveness. If you have unforgiveness or have done something wrong, repent. This step is very important for you must be clean before me in order to hear me.

(2) Bring into captivity any preconceived notions or ideas.

(3) Bring to captivity, any thought that would exalt itself above me, your Lord.

(4) Lay your flesh down, desiring only my will.

(5) Yield your spirit and soul to me, your Lord God.

(6) Claim this scripture: *My sheep listen to my voice; I know them, and they follow me. (John 10:27, NIV)* Claim you're my lamb and according to my word you are entitled to hear my voice.

(7) Ask your question. You will find that I speak to you with thoughts.

"Use this method for further revelations into my word. Also check with me if you feel hurt, take offense or need guidance. If you get a revelation and your not sure if it is mine or your own flesh, check with scripture."

"Dear friends, do not believe every spirit, but test the spirits to see whether they are from God, because many false prophets have gone out into the world. This is how you can recognize the Spirit of God: Every spirit that acknowledges that Jesus Christ has come in

the flesh is from God, but every spirit that does not acknowledge Jesus is not from God. This is the spirit of the antichrist, which you have heard is coming and even now is already in the world. You, dear children, are from God and have overcome them, because the one who is in you is greater than the one who is in the world." (1 John 4:1-4, NIV)

"Ask for a scripture to line up with my word. You will find, that I am faithful and love to give you revelations into my word. Learn I am a kind and merciful God. That I yearn to guide and lead you, yearn to communicate. If you will but exercise the faith of a little child, you will hear me. If you but lay your flesh down, you will hear me. If you lay aside your fears and any mistrust, you will hear me.

"You think, but he is the king of the universe, talking to me? Know this, I am the King but I am compassionate, and kind and you are my children.

"Use this lesson when asking for revelations of my scriptures. Check with me, 'when' and 'if' you take offense. Look to me and me alone, your Lord God, and you will truly sense my presence. I long to shoulder your cares, I long to be the most important thing in your life, nay, I demand it. Take this lesson as a gift from your Father."

"I am the good shepherd; I know my sheep and my sheep know me." (John 10:14, NIV)

"If any of you lacks wisdom, he should ask God, who gives generously to all without finding fault, and it will be given to him. But when he asks, he must believe and not doubt, because he who doubts is like a wave of the sea, blown and tossed by the wind. That man should not think he will receive anything from the Lord; he is a double-minded man, unstable in all he does." (James 1:5-8, NIV)

"When he has brought out all his own, he goes on ahead of them, and his sheep follow him because they know his voice." (John 10:4, NIV)

"No one knows when the bridegroom comes, but I, your Lord God give you another gem!

"If you live each day with the expectancy of seeing me coming down in the clouds in all my glory, you will not only live a life free of fear, but it will be free of worldly lusts. So says the Lord."

SECTION THREE

KNOW YOUR WEAPONS

Chapter Seven

GOD'S ARMOR

"Tho' there are many tribulations you yet face, if you face them with the surety and the knowledge that the gates of hell will not prevail, that I have you protected with a shield about you, it is only doubt that will allow the enemy to penetrate.

"Put forth your shield of faith and know it is a shield. Put forth your helmet of salvation and know it will protect your mind. Your breastplate of righteousness protects your heart. Your loins are protected with truth. Your feet are shod with the gospel of peace. The word of God is your sword. Read **Ephesians 6:10-18.**

"Do not just mouth these words, but know and understand they are truly spiritual armor. I say this, 'stand firm in tolerance, in truth, and in honesty. Be open but discrete. In all things give thanks for this is the will of God.' If you will remember my hand is upon you, my seal is upon you, my love is with you, WHAT DO YOU HAVE TO FEAR? So says your Lord."

Read: **Galations 2:20; Ephesians 1:13**

"When you put your armor on, it is as a protection. It protects from the fiery darts of the evil one, it protects you from the evil thought processes that are a part of your old nature. It also protects you against disease. However, you yourselves can open the door to illness by (1) sin, (2) unbelief, (3) accepting symptoms, and (4) entertaining evil thoughts. Example: Everyone has the flu, I hope I don't get it.

"Do you not see? If your spiritual armor is impenetrable and you believe, then how can you get sick? It says in my word you will tread upon serpents and not be harmed but, what if you tread and say, 'I hope I won't get hurt.' Do you not see the difference?"

Chapter Eight

FASTING

"The weapons we fight with are not the weapons of the world. On the contrary, they have divine power to demolish strongholds." (2 Corinthians 10:4, NIV)

"Fasting is a purification of the soul. It is a stripping away of oneself, in an unselfish manner. Its very powerful because it is a pure, unselfish act. It is a freeing, a putting down and a denial of the flesh. Fasting is powerful because, through the denial as you pray, there is no hindrance of self-indulgence. Fasting is another tool of spiritual warfare.

"When you fast and pray it is such a pure act of devotion, that the evil one and his cohorts cannot handle it. Hence, it takes fasting and prayer to get rid of some spirits. The power of fasting is mighty. It pulls down strongholds. It weakens long settled spirits and the prayer gets them out.

"Fasting is not to be taken lightly. It is deadly serious and very powerful. Fasting is an act of faith. A standing on my word. Its very power emanates through the spirit realm. There are times, when called to fast, the very act is a freeing. During a fast, you should be prayerful."

"When you fast, do not look somber as the hypocrites do, for they disfigure their faces to show men they are fasting. I tell you the truth, they have received their reward in full. But when you fast, put oil on your head and wash your face, so that it will not be obvious to men that you are fasting, but only to your Father, who is unseen; and your Father, who sees what is done in secret, will reward you." (Matthew 6:16-18, NIV)

"Pray throughout the day, lift your prayer unto me. Lock on the reason for the fast and lift that request up continually to me, during the fast.

"The purification of fasting is a blessing beyond your expectations. You find you hear my voice easier, you are more alert to my Spirit. Fasting is not to be used as a quick way to lose weight, but is to be approached with the purest of motives. I see the heart. It is the same with inner groaning, wailing and weeping if it is lead by my Spirit. It comes from your very depths. When that type of fast happens, for something or someone, its very power reaches directly to my throne room."

"He replied, Because you have so little faith. I tell you the truth, if you have faith as small as a mustard seed, you can say to this mountain, `Move from here to there' and it will move. Nothing will be impossible for you." (Matthew 17:20, NIV)

"The prayers of a righteous man availeth much. Never forget that if you are not called to fast, weep or travail, do not heap condemnation on yourself. Condemnation is not of me. I lead you each along different roads, or on different paths. One is not loved more than another."

"Where for forty days he was tempted by the devil. He ate nothing during those days, and at the end of them he was hungry." (Luke 4:2, NIV)

"Cornelius answered: "Four days ago I was in my house praying at this hour, at three in the afternoon. Suddenly a man in shining clothes stood before me and said, `Cornelius, God has heard your prayer and remembered your gifts to the poor." **(Acts 10:30-31, NIV)**

"In the same way, the Spirit helps us in our weakness. We do not know what we ought to pray for, but the Spirit himself intercedes for us with groans that words cannot express." **(Romans 8:26, NIV)**

Other scriptures: **Matthew 17:21; Acts 13:2-3; Acts 14:23;** and **Joel 2:12**

Chapter Nine

OUR RECOURSE

*"For our struggle is not against flesh and blood, but
against the rulers, against the authorities, against the
powers of this dark world and against the spiritual
forces of evil in the heavenly realms."*
(Ephesians 6:12, NIV)

"I will teach you to protect yourselves from the
onslaughts that are going to occur. Onslaughts, you say?
Yes, onslaughts. Onslaughts to your faith, onslaughts to
your health, onslaughts to your family, jobs, and income.
Onslaughts against everything you hold dear.

"One thing you must remember, I have not left you
weaponless. Look at the weapons I have given you; you
have not realized the importance of some of these weapons.

"The first and foremost recourse is:

A.   MY BLOOD...

"It paid the atonement for you."

*"And from Jesus Christ, who is the faithful witness, the
firstborn from the dead, and the ruler of the kings of*

*the earth. To him who loves us and has freed us from
our sins by his blood." (Revelation 1:5, NIV)*

"It was shed for you. It is also spiritually alive still,
because it is without sin to contaminate it, hence it is as
powerful now as when it was shed. When you are spiritually attacked plead my blood."

*"They overcame him by the blood of the Lamb and by
the word of their testimony; they did not love their
lives so much as to shrink from death."
(Revelation 12:11, NIV)*

"When you want protection, plead my blood. When you
are distraught and not knowing which direction to go, plead
my blood on your feet, so you will not make a move that is
not anointed. My blood is ever powerful as a protection. My
blood is the most powerful weapon of all, for my blood is
what defeated Satan in the first place. When you plead my
blood, do it with the knowledge that it works. Too many of
my children plead my blood by merely mouthing it.
However, if you will remember you are pleading my blood,
that I sacrificed for you and realize the power in that
statement, then your burdens lift off you for you have used,
one of my most effective tools, my blood. Know the purity
of my blood sends shivers unto the enemy, and the power
brings victory to my children who plead it with authority.

"So you can understand fully my blood, let me explain it
to you. My blood is pure and unblemished. Since it is so
pure and given with such love, it dispels all manner of
darkness. Love overcomes hate, goodness overcomes evil.

"My blood represents all my power and goodness and
love. Know and feel the truth of this. Get into your spirits
the purity and the clarity of my blood. Claim it and use it
and great miracles can and will happen. My blood is so pure
no evil can penetrate it. Know if you are washed in my
blood you can and will be mighty prayer warriors and intercessors.

"My blood was given freely, with no thought of myself but only my love for you. If you can comprehend even a little, the power in that love, this will come to light for you. Get into your spirits the magnificence of it, the blinding clarity of its power and you have a tool. A tool of divine origin, not to be taken lightly, but with reverence and awe.

B. MY WORD.

"I battled Satan by my word and you can also. When adversity comes at you on all sides, and you know not which way to turn, my word is a two—edged sword. The answers are there, so is the encouragement, the plans of salvation, plus all the guidance you can hope to receive. Do not forget, I am the same, today, yesterday and forever."

> *"Submit yourselves, then, to God. Resist the devil, and*
> *he will flee from you." (James 4:7, NIV)*

"You battle Satan effectively when you know my word. The spirit, buries my word inside, so know and have faith that if you but ask, he will bring it to memory. When you read my word, ask the Holy Spirit to file it away inside you. Know also, I do not let my warriors fall to the enemy. If I am for you, who is against you? If you will but realize the weapons you have, then you can rest in the knowledge and security of victory." Read: **Luke 4:3-13**

"If you will take the time to study my promises, then you too will have at hand a mighty tool. For example: You're confused, you feel you don't know which way to turn and you are full of fear, then speak into the spirit realm by saying, 'I refuse these symptoms because...'

> *"For God did not give us a spirit of timidity, but a spirit*
> *of power, of love and of self-discipline."*
> *(2 Timothy 1:7, NIV)*

'...then stand on that promise.' Another example is: you are tired of feeling weak, so tell the spirit realm, you can do

all things through Christ Jesus who strengthenths you.
Philippians. 4:13 You must speak them with conviction and
a surety that these are my promises to you."

C. THE ARMOR OF GOD.

> *"Therefore put on the full armor of God, so that when
> the day of evil comes, you may be able to stand your
> ground, and after you have done everything, to stand.
> Stand firm then, with the belt of truth buckled round
> your waist, with the breastplate of righteousness in
> place, and with your feet fitted with the readiness that
> comes from the gospel of peace. In addition to all this,
> take up the shield of faith, with which you can
> extinguish all the flaming arrows of the evil one. Take
> the helmet of salvation and the sword of the Spirit,
> which is the word of God. And pray in the Spirit on all
> occasions with all kinds of prayers and requests. With
> this in mind, be alert and always keep on praying for
> all the saints. " (Ephesians 6:13-18, NIV)*

"Never allow yourselves to go unarmed even for a
minute. The first thing you should do, when your feet hit
the floor is, put on the full armor of God so you can stand.
Many of you know this, but how many of you realize truly,
the importance of this? Putting your armor on should be as
automatic as getting dressed in the morning."

D. FAITH AND TRUST.

> *"For it is by grace you have been saved, through faith—
> and this not from yourselves, it is the gift of God. "
> (Ephesians 2:8, NIV)*

"You must learn to stand in faith, though all around you
seems as shambles. You have to believe I love you, believe
I am for you. Don't just say it, but feel it and know it so no
matter what happens you can stand in faith. When going
through difficult times, if you are joyful, you show the

world, and the spirit realm an undaunted spirit. It is a spirit who is in perfect harmony with me, when there is deep trust and you count adversity as joy. This is difficult at best; however, if you remember most trials, tests, and adversities have salvation or freeing behind them, it will help you to count it all as joy. Often the evil one is allowed to test you, for mighty blessings could be coming, and you will know it is in my strength that you stand, in my strength you overcome.

"If the trials you are going through is due to past sin, praise me there is a cleansing going on. When the flesh is laid down and my spirit rules and leads, there is nothing you cannot do. Faith moves mountains and so does trust in me. Do not look at circumstances, but beyond. Get your spirit eyes in focus. Those of you who are out in the world should know that serenity and peace show my light. Do not think others do not look at you for they do. Your reactions to things speak louder than words. If you are to utilize this weapon of faith and trust you must yield to me and me alone. That in turn allows my Spirit to guide, which in turn allows your faith and trust to blossom into full maturity."

E. PRAYER.

"Before you pray for someone, ask God, what he is doing in their lives. This is done in order to pray for God's perfect will."

"Therefore confess your sins to each other and pray for each other so that you may be healed. The prayer of a righteous man is powerful and effective."
(James 5:16, NIV)

"In the same way, the Spirit helps us in our weakness. We do not know what we ought to pray for, but the Spirit himself intercedes for us with groans that words cannot express." (Romans 8:26, NIV)

"Pray my protection, pray my anointing to flow over you, pray my intervention on your behalf. Do you not see? What good is prayer if not coupled with belief, with faith. Prayer and faith can move mountains. Hold on to my promise that I will direct you. Hold to my promise, I will not leave you orphaned, *'I will not leave you comfortless: I will come to you.' (John 14:18, NIV)*, hold to my promise that I will protect you. Never forget that you can be and are an overcomer in my strength."

"You, dear children, are from God and have overcome them, because the one who is in you is greater than the one who is in the world." (1 John 4:4, NIV)

F. ANOTHER WEAPON IS PRAISE.

"Why are you downcast, O my soul? Why so disturbed within me? Put your hope in God, for I will yet praise him, my Savior..." (Psalms 42:5, NIV)

"And sang the song of Moses the servant of God and the song of the Lamb: Great and marvelous are your deeds, Lord God Almighty. Just and true are your ways, King of the ages. Who will not fear you, O Lord, and bring glory to your name? For you alone are holy. All nations will come and worship before you, for your righteous acts have been revealed." (Revelation 15:3-4, NIV)

"Praise me when things seem to go wrong, praise me in all things."

"Contend, O LORD, with those who contend with me; fight against those who fight against me. Take up shield and buckler; arise and come to my aid. Brandish spear and javelin against those who pursue me. Say to my soul, "I am your salvation." May those who seek my life be disgraced and put to shame; may those who plot my ruin be turned back in dismay." (Psalms 35:1-4, NIV)

"Praise and song defeats the spirit of heaviness. Oh if you could only see how Satan hates praise and singing to me. Do you not realize that Satan was in charge of the heavenly choir? That he gnashes his teeth when song or dance breaks forth to my glory? Why else would Satan devise hard rock? Those beats are to his ominous glory."

G. FASTING

"Fasting is a weapon, sorely abused or neglected. Therefore, there is a separate lesson on fasting.

"Oh children, you are indeed in a battle. Have you ever wondered why you are called lambs? It is because so few of you realize the magnitude of the battle, so few of you realize what is at stake. Danger is everywhere you turn, and I, as the Good Shepherd guide, protect and keep you safe. I tell you all this, you must get into your hearts, once and for all.

(1) What the battle is for, it is for souls.
(2) Know what your weapons are.
(3) Know you have the victory if you but stand in faith and trust, using my weapons.

"Children, open your hearts and ears to this message. Open your eyes and realize the end is near. Stand and fight. Know your resources, know I have put my grace upon you, know I have defeated Satan so you can walk victoriously. But, most of all know and understand my love for you.

"Plead the blood, speak the word, stand in faith and trust, put your armor on, pray with your supplications, worship, sing, and dance unto me.

"If you do these things, you will find, not only the road to victory, but a victorious life. For those of you who put your trust in me, I will not disappoint. Those who put their cares on my shoulders, I will gladly carry. Those who give their lives to me, I give back life eternal.

"Know this and learn it well. I have already defeated the evil one. Those standing in my strength, on my word and putting their trust in me, along with their armor, and pleading with reverence my blood—need never fear.

"Know I see all heartaches, all circumstances and I say again to you:"

"Where is your faith? he asked his disciples. In fear and amazement they asked one another, Who is this? He commands even the winds and the water, and they obey him." (Luke 8:25, NIV)

"The LORD will fight for you; you need only to be still." (Exodus 14:14, NIV)

"Yet a time is coming and has now come when the true worshippers will worship the Father in spirit and truth, for they are the kind of worshippers the Father seeks.   God is spirit, and his worshippers must worship in spirit and in truth." (John 4:23-24, NIV)

"He replied, If you have faith as small as a mustard seed, you can say to this mulberry tree, `Be uprooted and planted in the sea,' and it will obey you." (Luke 17:6, NIV)

"Your word is a lamp to my feet and a light for my path." (Psalms 119:105, NIV)

Other scriptures are: **Proverbs 3:5-6; Hebrews 13:12-17; Luke 17:6-8; I Corinthians 11:25; Psalms 46:1-2; John 5:24; Deuteronomy 1:30**

Chapter Ten

THE ROAD OF A CHRISTIAN SOLDIER

"The road of a Christian soldier, is sometimes fraught with danger. There are many battles. Sometimes you feel all alone, like giving up. Yet, one little smile over a disappointment, one "praise the Lord" when you've been stuck with hurt, is victory.

"Angels line this road, clapping and cheering you on to victory. Sometimes they pick you up. I am the Almighty, the Deliverer and I am right beside you. You are **never** alone. Along the way, I provide rest, my word is the water and I give blessings. These blessings are encouragement.

"When you start on this road, you start slowly because you are often hampered by your pride, arrogance, addictions, fears or angers. These weigh heavy about you and are like chains.

"With the faith of a mustard seed, we start our walk. I always see the heart, the despair, joy, willingness or hopelessness, for I am starting this journey with you. The chains of the old you, the fears, and the low self-esteem start to drop off, as you go along this path. The walk gets **easier** and **narrower**.

"There are many fallen soldiers along the way, but know, the Christian walk is a walk 'of' and 'for' life. Never think the walk is not worth it for the reward is eternal life. Never think you can't go on, for I do not give nor allow, more than you can bear.

"All are not soldiers, all are not captains or generals. Know that even the babe, who starts on the road as a soldier, is my beloved and as dearly loved as the general, commanding many soldiers. Many times, through my love, I pick you up and carry you out of the valley. I set your feet straight and still the path narrows.

"The rewards are mighty, my children. The gifts are peace and serenity. The important thing to know and remember is, I am with you! So, live the victorious life!"

Chapter Eleven

A CALL TO ARMS

"I am calling to arms all my prayer warriors. What the enemy has stolen, must be taken back, what the enemy has meant for harm, I will turn to good if I have intercessors, if I have prayers.

"My spirit is not only being quenched, it is being stomped on and put out. I am calling my prayer warriors to put a stop to it, or there will be dire consequences. Consequences of shame, ridicule and the blasphemy of me, your God. Growth will stop, many will fall at Satan's hands. Do battle for me, war for me, raise up my prayer warriors, raise up the banner of the Lord, raise up my freedom, my hope and set the captives free in my strength.

"You are to unite with one purpose, one goal, one spirit, one reason, and that is to do my will, to do my bidding.

"If you and all my prayer warriors are faithful in this, then sit and watch miracles happen. Sit and watch my hand unfold and my spirit be unleashed and with that unleashing, captives will be set free.

"Do you think, I don't know what I'm asking? I'm asking for your faithfulness, I am asking your allegiance. So says your Lord."

"I ask you, therefore, not to be discouraged because of my sufferings for you, which are your glory. For this reason I kneel before the Father, from whom his whole family in heaven and on earth derives its name. I pray that out of his glorious riches he may strengthen you with power through his Spirit in your inner being, **(Ephesians 3:13-16, NIV)**

"Go and cry out to the gods you have chosen. Let them save you when you are in trouble!" **(Judges 10:14, NIV)**

"Not only so, but we also rejoice in our sufferings, because we know that suffering produces perseverance; perseverance, character; and character, hope. And hope does not disappoint us, because God has poured out his love into our hearts by the Holy Spirit, whom he has given us." **(Romans 5:3-5, NIV)**

"Strengthening the disciples and encouraging them to remain true to the faith. "We must go through many hardships to enter the kingdom of God," they said." **(Acts 14:22, NIV)**

Chapter Twelve

LIVING WITH AN UNBELIEVER

"If you are living with an unbeliever, who constantly invites the evil one in, you should remember, this is one of the reasons I say not to be harnessed to an unbeliever. For as oxen, if one is constantly pulling, in other words, has all the weight, will he not weaken? If one has all the burdens and the other does nothing will he not weaken? Yea, I say to you, it is only by my grace that a believer can endure with an unbeliever."

> *"Do not be yoked together with unbelievers. For what do righteousness and wickedness have in common? Or what fellowship can light have with darkness?"*
> *(2 Corinthians 6:14, NIV)*

"The goal should be to win the unbeliever to me, however it should be done by quietness of spirit and virtue. Chapter three in First Peter is good to read, regarding this. If however, the unbeliever continuously invites the evil one in, if that unbeliever wants to go, or leave the marriage, you must let them go."

> *"For the unbelieving husband has been sanctified through his wife, and the unbelieving wife has been sanctified through her believing husband. Otherwise your children would be unclean, but as it is, they are holy. But if the unbeliever leaves, let him do so. A believing man or woman is not bound in such circumstances; God has called us to live in peace." (1 Corinthians 7:14-15, NIV)*

"This is a war. Through each trial, through each tribulation, if you can give God glory, give God praise, then you will be victorious.

"Do not underestimate the importance of your lights, do not underestimate your adversary or let down your guard, but stand in truth, stand in the Lord's light, in the Lord's strength."

SECTION FOUR

LET THE
OLD NATURE DIE

Chapter

Thirteen

WHY WE SHOULD
DIE TO SELF

*"For God so loved the world that he gave his one
and only Son that whoever believes in him shall not
perish but have eternal life. For God did not send
his Son into the world to condemn the world, but to
save the world through him. Whoever believes in
him is not condemned, but whoever does not believe
stands condemned already because he has not
believed in the name of God's one and only Son."
(John 3:16-18, NIV)*

"I am saying that all those that believe, truly believe are
not the same person, for when you walk in light (with me)
does not light dispel darkness? If so, how can any who say
they believe in me, not change? The problem is that Satan
goes to work overtime to dull the senses, to puff up my
people, to tell them, 'you believe in Jesus, you go to church,
you are saved, but I say to you, is that all there is? Is that
not what is meant by lukewarm?"

"I know your deeds, that you are neither cold nor hot. I wish you were either one or the other!   So, because you are lukewarm—neither hot nor cold—I am about to spit you out of my mouth." (Revelation 3:15-16, NIV)

"Look to me in all things, I am not only interested, I yearn to be included. Ask! Those of you who live my word, read my word, commune with me in prayer, you are my people."

"Let us acknowledge the LORD; let us press on to acknowledge him. As surely as the sun rises, he will appear; he will come to us like the winter rains, like the spring rains that water the earth." (Hosea 6:3, NIV)

"I did not die part way, I did not take just a little of your sins upon me, I died, tasted hell, was victorious over it, got the keys to heaven and hell, had all, unequivocally all, your sins laid upon me."

"I am the Living One; I was dead, and behold I am alive for ever and ever! And I hold the keys of death and Hades." (Revelation 1:18, NIV)

"When you accept me as your savior, you are no longer the same. I say to you, all of you, you must forbear, and you must continue walking close to me, for the fowler is there to steal your joy."

"Since you have kept my command to endure patiently, I will also keep you from the hour of trial that is going to come upon the whole world to test those who live on the earth. I am coming soon. Hold on to what you have, so that no-one will take your crown.
(Revelation 3:10-11, NIV)

"Ask my guidance, I willingly give it. Truly seek and you shall find. Be prepared, stand on my promises."

*"So I say to you: Ask and it will be given to you; seek
and you will find; knock and the door will be opened
to you." (Luke 11:9, NIV)*

*"I say in my word that because you are lukewarm—
neither hot nor cold—I am about to spit you out of my
mouth. (Revelation 3:16, NIV)*

"You will say but Lord, we knew you and, I will say I
knew you not. "Do you not see? If you know me, then you
desire to be more like me; if you know me, you desire to
know me more; if you know me, you desire to please me,
commune with me, and defer to me. In other words, by
those simple things you grow, and you change. You cannot
do all the dark things. You step out into the light. You walk
in peace, you walk in harmony, you look to me, instead of
man."

*"Neither do people light a lamp and put it under a
bowl. Instead they put it on its stand, and it gives light
to everyone in the house. In the same way, let your
light shine before men, that they may see your good
deeds and praise your Father in heaven."
(Matthew 5:15-16, NIV)*

"I say to you, to know me is to love me for I have first
loved you. Commit all things to me. Did I die for you, only
to harm you? Know you foolish children, I am your Father,
I love you, I discipline you because I love you. Do you not
see? I see the greater plan. This life is but for a twinkling of
the eye, but I prepare a place for you for eternity. I prepare a
place of peace, of joy and happiness."

*"Do not store up for yourselves treasures on earth,
where moth and rust destroy, and where thieves break
in and steal. But store up for yourselves treasures in
heaven, where moth and rust do not destroy, and where
thieves do not break in and steal." (Matthew 6:19-20, NIV)*

"I ask you now, each of you, recommit your lives to me. Ask me to help you to surrender all to me. Ask me into your lives, all parts of your lives. Do not just mouth it, do not be luke warm, for woe be unto you.

"These are the last days and I am calling my people. Stand fast, ever true. The rewards far outweigh the cost. Come to me and allow me to teach you, allow me to help you, for when you surrender all to me, you are not in the way and you can receive my full blessings.

"Peruse this, meditate on this. These are my promises, I, your Lord God, give you. Fight the good fight, keep your lamps lit, it is later then you think."

"Those whom I love I rebuke and discipline. So be earnest, and repent. Here I am! I stand at the door and knock. If anyone hears my voice and opens the door, I will come in and eat with him, and he with me. To him who overcomes, I will give the right to sit with me on my throne, just as I overcame and sat down with my Father on his throne. He who has an ear, let him hear what the Spirit says to the churches."
(Revelation 3:19-22, NIV)

"I know your deeds. See, I have placed before you an open door that no one can shut. I know that you have little strength, yet you have kept my word and have not denied my name. I will make those who are of the synagogue of Satan, who claim to be Jews though they are not, but are liars—I will make them come and fall down at your feet and acknowledge that I have loved you. Since you have kept my command to endure patiently, I will also keep you from the hour of trial that is going to come upon the whole world to test those who live on the earth. I am coming soon. Hold on to what you have, so that no one will take your crown. Him who overcomes I will make a pillar in the temple of my God. Never again will he leave it. I will write on him the name of my God and the name of the city of my God, the new Jerusalem, which is coming

down out of heaven from my God; and I will also write on him my new name.   He who has an ear, let him hear what the Spirit says to the churches." (Rev. 3:8-13, NIV)

"Let us acknowledge the Lord; let us press on to acknowledge him.   As surely as the sun rises, he will appear; he will come to us like the winter rains, like the spring rains that water the earth." (Hosea 6:3, NIV)

Chapter Fourteen

SURRENDER

"In order to let the Holy Spirit take control (die to self). Remember to defer to me in all things, large and small. I am interested in the minutest detail of your lives.

"I see your thoughts, your fears, your unconcern and your concerns. If I am to mold you into the 'you' I created, I need you not only yielded, but seeking my guidance in all things. You see children, I not only see into the darkest recesses of your heart, but I see your thoughts as well. That is why I am and can always work changes in each of you, for you all fall short of my glory."

"If any of you lacks wisdom, he should ask God, who gives generously to all without finding fault, and it will be given to him." (James 1:5, NIV)

"To die to oneself is to give up and surrender all to me. To die to oneself is to empty yourself in preparation for a total indwelling in all areas of your life. To die to oneself is to totally, not only surrender yourself and your family but to desire only my will. To die unto oneself brings rewards only a few experience."

"... and to put on the new self, created to be like God in true righteousness and holiness." (Ephesians 4:24, NIV)

"When you relinquish your hold on your children, pets, work, when you surrender evil thoughts, all or any resentments, when you at last come to that point of desiring my will over yours, miracles happen. You walk in peace and contentment and with a joy before unknown to you, for you then walk in the perfect will of the Father. To die to oneself, takes faith and great love. If you truly want this, then all blessings will flow. Walk in my light, walk in my love, search me out in any small area of your life. Check yourself, get and keep yourself pure before me."

"Search me, O God, and know my heart; test me and know my anxious thoughts. See if there is any offensive way in me, and lead me in the way everlasting." (Psalms 139:23-24, NIV)

"Dying to oneself is totally giving up everything to my care, trusting in me completely to look after you. You are a new creature in Christ when you accept me. You have new hope, bondage is broken constantly, you are drawn closer to me. You have died to self, yet the deeper meaning of dying to self is **the conscious, voluntary giving of literally all in your life.**"

"Therefore, if anyone is in Christ, he is a new creation; the old has gone, the new has come!"
(2 Corinthians 5:17, NIV)

"Take heart, for this is not impossible, even though you live in a world of wealth, lust, and perversion. You and each of you can make this a conscious goal.

"My word says, 'in all things trust in the Lord your God and lean not to thine own understanding and he will direct your path.' Do you not see the meaning now?"

"Trust in the LORD with all your heart and lean not on your own understanding; in all your ways acknowledge him, and he will make your paths straight." (Proverbs 3:5-6, NIV)

"It is possible to truly die to self, while living in this world, but not in your own strength or will. Ask me to help, for all things are made possible by me. I am more than willing to not only lead, but direct your path in dying to self. Each day, ask me to help. Surrendering your will leads to a tranquility you have never before experienced. It leads to a faith unshakable, it leads to a peace that passeth all understanding."

"I will instruct you and teach you in the way you should go; I will counsel you and watch over you." (Psalms 32:8, NIV)

"Stand and receive for my blessings pour down, stand and receive my anointing oils. I, your Lord God, bless you. I, your Lord God, look after you. I, your Lord God, love every hair on your head. I, your Lord God, protect you. It is so."

"Jesus looked at them and said, 'With man this is impossible, but with God all things are possible.'" (Matthew 19:26, NIV)

Chapter Fifteen

SUBMISSION

"Serve one another. Serving my poor will bring forth blessings, however, there is to be a deferring of oneself, not out of rejection, not out of low self-esteem, not out of the sense of unworthiness but with a joy, with a peace. See you not? To walk in the spirit or die to self, means having pure motives."

> *"Do not lie to each other, since you have taken off your old self with its practices and have put on the new self, which is being renewed in knowledge in the image of its Creator." (Colossians 3:9-10, NIV)*

"In all things, I see your motives. Why you take offense, why you feel hurt, why you stay away from someone, why you are always with someone else.

"Let's take the first. Why do certain things offend you? Why do certain things bother you more than others? Is it because of past hurts, fears or misunderstanding? What is it about your hurts or circumstances that has made you fearful? The solution lies in looking to me rather then man.

You must do as I have told you. Check with me, regarding criticism or scorn. If there is truth in any criticism received, repent, ask my help in overcoming it. That is part of dying to self, looking to me rather than man.

"Staying away from someone, avoiding them, for no good reason is an example of taking offense to the extreme and being judgemental. Does it not say in my word, to love one another? If you stay away from someone because they're different, because you don't like them, check your motives."

"Then we will no longer be infants, tossed back and forth by the waves, and blown here and there by every wind of teaching and by the cunning and craftiness of men in their deceitful scheming. Instead, speaking the truth in love, we will in all things grow up into him who is the Head, that is, Christ." (Ephesians 4:14-15, NIV)

"If you are, on the other hand, always with one person, always seeking out your group, check your motives. Have they become idols to you? I will not tolerate idols in your life. It says in my word, go and evangelize the world, you too can go and evangelize. In your group of acquaintances, seek out the stragglers, look to the lonely, see if you can bring my light to the forlorn, to the 'odd' person. When you meet strangers on buses, in restaurants, or on your job, let my light shine through you. That is the way to evangelize.

"Walking in the spirit, or dying to self means just that. Remember you are sojourners, here but for a little while. Do all things for my glory. Check to see if it will glorify my Son, Christ Jesus.

"I tell you this, if you can gain an understanding of 'dying to self,' you will find such freedom, such joy, such peace. You will no longer have to live with hurt feelings, with rejection, with low self-esteem. Do you not see the freeing here? If you walk with eyes towards me, not man, if you put your trust in me, not man, if you look to glorify me, not self, you will experience a true freeing. Never forget, greater is He who is in you, then he who is in this world.

Walk my path, straight and true
let your light shine through,
for peace and freedom awaits you there
freedom from hurts, freedom from care.

For you will walk along with me
and I will give you eyes that see,
my blessings and miracles that abound
and you will find, its peace you've found.

"Many walk with blinders of hurt, not seeing that unforgiveness only breeds more hurt. Many walk with such blinders in their own lives. Even when doing my work, they are unaware of their own shortcomings. You have been given this insight to teach you to not only walk in forgiveness and love, but also to walk without judging. The evil forces abound everywhere but those that diligently seek me, find me. You are my 'lights,' you must keep your lamps lit for the time draws near. I would gather my bride to me. Spread my word for the time grows short, 'I return soon.'

"I want you all to always walk aware of the 'logs' in your own eyes. Walk in uprightness, honesty and truth. Do not allow malicious mischief a foothold. Remember, I surround thee, I protect thee, so keep on. The road has been straightened before you, the dark has been kept away. Remember my goals, and keep them foremost before you."

"Finally, be strong in the Lord and in his mighty power." (Ephesians 6:10, NIV)

"Now it is required that those who have been given a trust must prove faithful." (1 Corinthians 4:2, NIV)

Chapter Sixteen

TRUST

"Upholding one another foils the evil one's plans. He would cause division, I, unity. He would cause strife, I peace. He would cause chaos, I, tranquility. Dying to self is a way of easing all pain for your complete trust is in me. Dying to self brings forth rewards unexpected, along with blessings. Do you not see? If each day you truly place all in my care, where is the worry, where is the anxiety?"

"Who of you by worrying can add a single hour to his life?" (Matthew 6:27, NIV)

"Dying to self does not insulate you from care, but you are more open and you can hand me the worry and care before they can attach themselves to you."

"Cast all your anxiety on him because he cares for you. Be self-controlled and alert. Your enemy the devil prowls around like a roaring lion looking for someone to devour. Resist him, standing firm in the faith, because you know that your brothers throughout the

*world are undergoing the same kind of sufferings. And
the God of all grace, who called you to his eternal
glory in Christ, after you have suffered a little while,
will himself restore you and make you strong, firm and
steadfast. To him be the power for ever and ever.
Amen." (1 Peter 5:7-11, NIV)*

"Do you not see? Dying to self actually makes you more
open to other's sorrows, more open to their hurt, to a care,
and a love of your fellow man. You must learn to give your
thoughts, your trust, your cares, your worries to me before
doubt, anxiety or guilt can take hold. This is a freeing
beyond your belief. So when you fall short, your intimate
knowledge of me, will assure you of forgiveness, so Satan
cannot rob your joy."

*"If we confess our sins, he is faithful and just and
will forgive us our sins and purify us from all
unrighteousness." (1 John 1:9, NIV)*

"There is profound truth here. Read and read again.
There is much to be gleaned. Ask my Holy Spirit to help
you grasp the truth's inner meaning; to really grab hold of
the truth. This is not an impossible way, it is not unattainable
for like all my requests, all my lessons, and all my teachings
have simplicity in themselves. All of you can achieve this,
all can attain it, but you must desire it."

*"Finally, be strong in the Lord and in his mighty
power." (Ephesians 6:10, NIV)*

"You must be prepared, for times of adversity are near.
That is why you should "die to self" for you are my valiant
soldiers. Read my word, practice, practice and practice it.
March together in camaraderie and brotherhood. Uphold,
uplift one another for the lion seeks those who he can
devour.

"Learn this, I am invincible, I am the victor. Do not
focus on difficult circumstances, but stand, knowing all is
not as it seems."

"I tell you the truth, you will weep and mourn while the world rejoices. You will grieve, but your grief will turn to joy." (John 16:20, NIV)

"As you practice and die to self, you grow very strong in me, so much that you can laugh at adversity for you will be safe and secure in the knowledge that I, your Lord God, will not let you fall!"

"Not only so, but we also rejoice in our sufferings, because we know that suffering produces perse - verance; perseverance, character; and character, hope. And hope does not disappoint us, because God has poured out his love into our hearts by the Holy Spirit, whom he has given us." (Romans 5:3-5, NIV)

"Rejoice in your lessons, for they are freeing. Rejoice when your faith gets stretched. Rejoice in all things and you have another key to my kingdom. Never allow fear to take hold for it is from the enemy. Never allow anxiety in, for it is a way the enemy uses to get a foothold. Nay, I say to you, stand upright for I am victorious."

"The death he died, he died to sin once for all; but the life he lives, he lives to God. In the same way, count yourselves dead to sin but alive to God in Christ Jesus. Therefore do not let sin reign in your mortal body so that you obey its evil desires. Do not offer the parts of your body to sin, as instruments of wickedness, but rather offer yourselves to God, as those who have been brought from death to life; and offer the parts of your body to him as instruments of righteousness. For sin shall not be your master, because you are not under law, but under grace. (Romans 6:10-14, NIV)

Note: See writings on trust in the lessons on anxiety.
Romans 5; 1 Peter 5 (NIV)

Chapter Seventeen

SPIRIT EYES
(Seeing things through spiritual discernment)

"Learn to look beyond circumstances, beyond hassles, and beyond tribulation. Focus your spirit eyes. When you do, it provides not only an understanding, but a release of tension, a release from anxiety. Focusing your spirit eyes, takes a knowledge and an understanding of who I am and how loving I am."

> *"And we know that in all things God works for the good of those who love him, who have been called according to his purpose." (Romans 8:28, NIV)*

"My ways are not your ways. I can turn tragedy to good and I can use tribulation as a learning process. Therefore, ask my Spirit to help you focus your 'spirit eyes' on 'why' something is happening and what lesson is in it for you.

"Sometimes, someone's illness can only be seen as suffering. Yet, if you focus your spirit eyes, you can find many people touched by that illness, as they witness my glory on that person. That is one of the highest forms of witnessing...when you are ill and still praising me. You must remember that the time spent here is but for a twinkling of the eye."

"So we fix our eyes not on what is seen, but on what is unseen. For what is seen is temporary, but what is unseen is eternal." **(2 Corinthians 4:18, NIV)**

"The end times are near. How better can this time be spent than in glorifying me, witnessing for me. All of you should feed my poor and give them clothes, for whatever you do for the poor is a witness to me."

"He who gives to the poor will lack nothing, but he who closes his eyes to them receives many curses." **(Proverbs 28:27, NIV)**

"Focusing your spirit eyes brings blessings and draws us closer for you start to understand me and my ways a little better, thus you are drawn yet closer.

"The poor are also the poor in spirit. Take care that each day is uplifted to me, that each day you invite me to have full reign in your life and that each day you lay your flesh and your will down. Invite me to have my will done in your life. As you do this, focusing your spirit eyes becomes easier. It, like anything else, needs to be practiced."

"When he has brought out all his own, he goes on ahead of them, and his sheep follow him because they know his voice." **(John 10:4, NIV)**

"When an event happens, that seems to have no answer, ask me to help you focus your spirit eyes. Where the scriptures say, I go after the straying sheep, it refers, not only to those who have turned their back to me, but those who have walked out from the shelter of my arms. That is where your spirit eyes will help you. Focus them upon a situation, see if there is any danger there or if there are pitfalls. When you grow and become more mature, not only is more expected of you but snares and traps are everywhere. Hence you must walk close, else you will become ensnared."

> *"He lifted me out of the slimy pit, out of the mud and mire; he set my feet on a rock and gave me a firm place to stand." (Psalms 40:2, NIV)*

"Do you not see? A good check point in decision making is, 'how would Jesus feel, what would Jesus do?' and yield to me, not only in words, but in deeds.

"The lesson here is to treat everyone as you would like to be treated. If someone is surly or unkind, focus your spirit eyes and see why. If you cannot see the reason, then walk in my love, compassion, and forgiveness and pray for them. Sometimes little one, it takes a deep hurt or a shock to learn a lesson.

"Spirit eyes is a treasure of mine that's yours for the asking, for the pursuing. With this precious gift comes peace, understanding, tolerance, and patience. Spirit eyes allow you to see my hand upon a situation. Sometimes our children, other people, circumstances or situations have to come to a crises for you to cry, 'Help me, Abba Father.' There are also times when circumstances seem inexplicably sorrowful; yet, you must remember, I desire all things to my glory. There may also be times when past hurts must be healed before restoration comes, before a total healing of body and the circumstance comes.

"I am never impatient. When things seem to drag on, praise me, for I am testing and teaching you. Never forget, when you became born again, spirit filled, and ask me to totally work in your life, you will join my army. The battle is very real. That is why it is important for my warriors to have prayers and good samaritans to lift them up when they fall down. The uniqueness of my army is, it has already defeated the foe. Your tests are of faithfulness and endurance, for the prize is life eternal in joy, harmony and peace."

"He will reply, I tell you the truth, whatever you did not do for one of the least of these, you did not do for me." **(Matthew 25:45, NIV)**

"Ears that hear and eyes that see—the LORD has made them both." **(Proverbs 20:12, NIV)**

Chapter Eighteen

EARS TO HEAR

"I would teach your ears to hear what the Spirit has to say. To have ears that hear takes a willingness to lay down pre-conceived notions. Too many of my people have their minds closed. Closed from reading other interpretations, closed from not checking with me. Too many think, 'that person hears from the Lord, so all things they say are from me, your Lord.' For example: a minister or an evangelist you hear on the radio, or television, even your minister are not 100% right on; yet, some of my people say, 'So and so said it, so it must be right.'"

"Dear friends, do not believe every spirit, but test the spirits to see whether they are from God, because many false prophets have gone out into the world. This is how you can recognize the Spirit of God: Every spirit that acknowledges that Jesus Christ has come in the flesh is from God, but every spirit that does not acknowledge Jesus is not from God. This is the spirit of the antichrist, which you have heard is coming and even now is already in the world. You, dear children,

are from God and have overcome them, because the one who is in you is greater than the one who is in the world." (1 John 4:1-4, NIV)

"I would have each of you learn to check with me. Search the scriptures. It is your job, each of you, to check everything out, lest the deceiver slip in. Therefore, having spiritual ears is more then hearing my voice, it includes searching the scriptures, seeking the truth."

"So I say to you: Ask and it will be given to you; seek and you will find; knock and the door will be opened to you." (Luke 11:9, NIV)

"I say to each of you, the only true and living source is my bible. If it is not in the bible, discard it. Ask the Holy Spirit to sharpen your ears to actually know in your spirit, what is from God and what is not. To hear and sharpen your ears, takes listening and practice. Be still before me each day. Do you not realize, I truly desire to communicate with you, to be part of your life, to be considered in all you do or say? Am I only a God to come to during times of trouble? Am I as a filthy dish rag, to be used and then discarded?"

"For evildoers shall be cut off: but those that wait upon the LORD, they shall inherit the earth." (Psalms 37:9, NIV)

"Listen to this parable. There once was a man who was a kind giving person. He loved so much and was seeking one to love him back. As he was walking and contemplating this, he heard cries of distress. He rushed to see what was happening and there was a woman, weeping and forlorn. She had been abandoned by her friends and family. The kind man lifted her up, comforted her, looked after her, helped her wounds to heal and gave her riches beyond her dreams. He told her that he loved her. Yet, as soon as her wounds were healed, as soon as she started to feel better, she left the kind man's home, not even saying "thank you" or "good-bye". She went off with her friends again, the ones who had rejected her, to her family who had spurned her, and went right back to the filth and dirt from which she came.

"Is it any different with any of you? Do you not cry out to me in your calamity and then promptly forget me until you need me again? **Do I mean so little to you?**"

> *"... turning your ear to wisdom and applying your heart to understanding, and if you call out for insight and cry aloud for understanding, and if you look for it as for silver and search for it as for hidden treasure, then you will understand the fear of the LORD and find the knowledge of God. For the LORD gives wisdom, and from his mouth come knowledge and understanding. He holds victory in store for the upright, he is a shield to those whose walk is blameless, for he guards the course of the just and protects the way of his faithful ones. Then you will understand what is right and just and fair—every good path. (Proverbs 2:2-9, NIV)*

"Yet, I wait every day for you to communicate with me, allowing me to become an integral part of your lives. I long to heal, to talk, to bless each of you. Will you not tarry with me? Have your ears turned to me? You see love is patient, love is kind, never demanding, always forgiving. Know I yearn for your love and to be allowed to show my love. Ask me for ears that hear, ask me to come and live with you, to be a part of you and I will."

> *"No-one whose hope is in you will ever be put to shame, but they will be put to shame who are treacherous without excuse." (Psalms 25:3, NIV)*

> *"Look to the LORD and his strength; seek his face always." (Psalms 105:4, NIV)*

> *"Son of man, you are living among a rebellious people. They have eyes to see but do not see and ears to hear but do not hear, for they are a rebellious people." (Ezekiel 12:2, NIV)*

Chapter Nineteen

WALKING IN PEACE

"If you want to walk in love always, if you want to walk in my strength, if you truly wish to walk in the spirit and die to self, here are some guidelines to help you, not only get there, but to see the wisdom, blessings and by–product."

"Blessed are the peacemakers, for they will be called sons of God." (Matthew 5:9, NIV)

"Why do you look at the speck of sawdust in your brother's eye and pay no attention to the plank in your own eye?" (Matthew 7:3, NIV)

"If you are to walk in peace, take your eyes off self. That is one of the guidelines. If you are to walk in peace, promoting peace, you cannot walk in judgement, nor in condemnation."

"Therefore there is now no condemnation for those who are in Christ Jesus" (Romans 8:1, NIV).

"Making peace and walking in peace, blesses everyone with whom you come in contact. It is my way, the way you should walk. A guideline for walking the way of peace and the Spirit is, not taking offense. If someone speaks harshly to you, criticizes you, takes advantage of you, then ask me to help you see what may be the cause and if there is any truth in the criticism. If there is, thank them for bringing it to your attention. That is the gentle way, the peacemaker's way. You can also say, I'll check with God, thanks for bringing it to my attention.

"Dear ones, don't you see, if you could all just do that, how much heartache you could spare yourselves? If you did these simple things then rejection and low self-esteem would once and for all be defeated in your lives. For you would be looking to me, rather than to man for your affirmation. Ponder and meditate on this and you will experience a magnitude of freeing.

"If you walk the way of peace, taking no offense, you become an effective tool. The brighter your light shines, the more people will notice and wonder what it is that makes you so different. Others will begin to want 'what you have.' In this way, you also defeat selfishness, for the walk of peace is thinking of others, their comfort, their needs, and requirements other than your own. If you walk always thinking of others, your own actions will not bring harm, create havoc or unintentional hurt to anyone. There are many innocent victims of another person's transgressions.

"Many of these victims are innocent of their own, but by somehow being connected in some way to the transgressors, many have had to carry the transgressor's shame, and the transgressor's punishment. There are endless examples, like innocent children born into homes where they are molested or beaten; felons and breakers of the law...what about their spouses and children? Alcoholics, what of the havoc they create? Men like the Nazis, how many innocent were victimized? Oh, don't you see now?

"If you walk the way of peace, you walk not only on my road, but you walk past snares and traps. That is not to say, you yourself cannot become an innocent victim, but trust in me my children. I turn all things to good."

"And we know that in all things God works for the good of those who love him, who have been called according to his purpose." (Romans 8:28, NIV)

"Stand the test, stand the fire. "

"Therefore, brothers, we have an obligation—but it is not to the sinful nature, to live according to it. For if you live according to the sinful nature, you will die; but if by the Spirit you put to death the misdeeds of the body, you will live, because those who are led by the Spirit of God are sons of God. For you did not receive a spirit that makes you a slave again to fear, but you received the Spirit of sonship. And by him we cry, "Abba, Father. The Spirit himself testifies with our spirit that we are God's children. Now if we are children, then we are heirs—heirs of God and co-heirs with Christ, if indeed we share in his sufferings in order that we may also share in his glory. I consider that our present sufferings are not worth comparing with the glory that will be revealed in us. The creation waits in eager expectation for the sons of God to be revealed." (Romans 8:12-19, NIV)

"The important thing is as you walk the road of peace, you will not become a transgressor, causing other innocent people hurt. You will also be able to walk in forgiveness if you have been victimized, because you are responsible to me. Do not forget, vengeance is mine."

"He must turn from evil and do good; he must seek peace and pursue it." (1 Peter 3:11, NIV)

"Do not take revenge, my friends, but leave room for God's wrath, for it is written: "It is mine to avenge; I will repay," says the Lord. (Romans 12:19, NIV)

"Walking the way of peace is not only my way, but it leads you spiritually closer to me. Then, I become more in you and you become less, therefore 'dying to self.' When this happens, blessings abound beyond your imagination, for you will be able to see more and more through your 'spirit eyes.' You will be able to see beyond your current circumstances. You will be able to stand tests, trials, and tribulations with a peace and knowledge that I direct your path and will never leave you nor forsake you."

> *"Keep your lives free from the love of money and be content with what you have, because God has said, Never will I leave you; never will I forsake you."*
> *(Hebrews 13:5, NIV)*

"This is attainable because it is simple. All it takes is turning your eyes towards me, away from man, away from circumstances and trust in me."

> *"Trust in the LORD with all your heart and lean not on your own understanding; in all your ways acknowledge him, and he will make your paths straight." (Proverbs 3:5-6, NIV)*

Chapter Twenty

LAYING THE FLESH DOWN

"The laying down of flesh is done daily by (1) dedicating each day to me, (2) allowing me to work in every situation in your life, and (3) trusting me, by letting your walls of resistance down. This is also the way that faith grows."

"You, however, are controlled not by the sinful nature but by the Spirit, if the Spirit of God lives in you. And if anyone does not have the Spirit of Christ, he does not belong to Christ." (Romans 8:9, NIV)

"To allow me to work in all areas of your life requires complete trust. A complete knowledge that I would never hurt you. A trust so great that the revelation of hurtful incidents, and hurtful things you have done, or exposing areas of your personality that are not pleasing to me, is welcome. In this, you can rejoice. I never reveal sin to hurt you, but to free you."

"and have put on the new self, which is being renewed in knowledge in the image of its Creator."
(Colossians 3:10, NIV)

"Who is he that condemns? Christ Jesus, who died—
more than that, who was raised to life—is at the right
hand of God and is also interceding for us."
(Romans 8:34, NIV)

"Get an understanding of this, store it in your hearts.
When it gets settled in deeply, it, along with the inner
knowledge that all is done 'with' and 'in' love, you can truly
start laying the flesh down.
    (1)   Daily lift yourselves to me.
    (2)   In all things, allow me to work my work in you.
This is done with practice. Practice it in every situation until
it becomes second nature to you. For instance, 'Father,
should I buy this or not?' 'Father, should I stay home or
not?' 'Not my will but thine.'"

"Are you so foolish? After beginning with the Spirit, are
you now trying to attain your goal by human effort?"
(Galatians 3:3, NIV)

"As you practice these two steps, it will become second
nature to you, and will diligently lead you to victory. If you
ask me for guidance, in all situations, and you follow that
guidance, you begin to discover a sense of well-being that
comes from being in my will. Peace and serenity come even
in times of trouble, for you will look beyond the time of
trouble to the ultimate goal. Can you not see how this works
my children? It means, start each day by giving it to me,
yielding to me in all things, and it will bring you peace.
Faith and trust are so abounding, you can move mountains.
Faith is so steadfast you will wonder at the simplicity of it,
yet know how awesome it is."

"Praise be to the Lord, for he has heard my cry for
mercy. The LORD is my strength and my shield; my
heart trusts in him, and I am helped. My heart leaps
for joy and I will give thanks to him in song. The Lord
is the strength of his people, a fortress of salvation for

his anointed one. Save your people and bless your inheritance; be their shepherd and carry them for ever." (Psalms 28:6-9, NIV)

"In all things, give thanks. In all things, lift praises up to me. Know I am interested in the smallest, minutest detail. Know I long to bless you, comfort you and guide you."

"Those who belong to Christ Jesus have crucified the sinful nature with its passions and desires. Since we live by the Spirit, let us keep in step with the Spirit. Let us not become conceited, provoking and envying each other." (Galatians 5:24-26, NIV)

"Get a spiritual understanding of the simplicity of this. Open your hearts, my children. Be willing and miracles will happen; miracles of faith, growth, peace and serenity.

"Be ever alert and on guard. When you lift yourself and your problems to me in prayer, know and understand the meaning. Do not just mouth the words, get the meaning into your heart, feel the yielding, rest in the secure knowledge that you are nestled in my wings, and arms. Practice this until it becomes as second nature. This is a new dimension in your spiritual walk, a new closeness.

"If you truly dedicate your life to me, you will be free from worries, for you will see beyond the trial or current circumstances. You will have no needs go unmet. Did I not give manna from Heaven to mine in the wilderness? Do you think you are any less? Do I love you any less? Be still and know... really know, that I am the Lord God Almighty."

"And to put on the new self, created to be like God in true righteousness and holiness." (Ephesians 4:24, NIV)

Chapter
Twenty-One

TROUBLED TIMES

"There are times in everyone's life, when they don't know what to do, or more importantly they can't do anything themselves about the circumstances in which they find themselves. Sometimes it's a hole they have dug for themselves, sometimes it is circumstances beyond their control. When this happens, some turn to me for solace, aid and help while others walk away from me, saying, 'it's God's fault they have cancer, are in debt, or that a loved one has left.' That is one of the reasons it is called the refiner's fire or breaking of one.(**Malachi 3:3, NIV**)

"The first choice, of course, is to turn toward or away from me. If you turn toward me, and if you are being refined, you are being brought to a state of total dependence on me. In this way only, can you say with conviction, 'do with me what you will.' It is, in this broken state, you can be brought close to me; in this broken state that you can be used. I see the greater plan, I see the circumstances, full and complete to their conclusion. How much heartache everyone could save if everyone would say, 'What are you teaching me Lord? What do you want of my life? Take it, its yours to do with as you wish.' Do you not see the final breaking taking place?

"Nature, as it is however, lets you get on your feet. Then the old man arises and again you must be broken or else you will be drawn back into the world's ways. It is my love that breaks you, it is my love which helps you to succeed, it is my love that heals, guides and directs.

"I would have you get on your knees. Offer me not only your all, but give me yourselves to do with as I wish. Then, if you do this, trust, rejoice and have faith that all will be in my hands, and in my plans. Realize my love."

> *"Arise, shine, for your light has come, and the glory of the Lord rises upon you. See, darkness covers the earth and thick darkness in over the people, but the Lord rises upon you and his glory appears over you. Nations will come to your light, and kings to the brightness of your dawn. Lift up your eyes and look about you: All assemble and come to you; your sons come from afar, and your daughters are carried on the arm." (Isaiah 60:1-4, NIV)*

> *"You are taught, with regard to your former way of life, to put off your old self, which is being corrupted by its deceitful desires; to be made new in the attitude of your minds; and to put on the new self, created to be like God in true righteousness and holiness. Therefore, each of you must put off falsehood and speak truthfully to his neighbor, for we are all members of one body." (Ephesians 4:22-25, NIV)*

> *"Those who look to him are radiant; their faces are never covered with shame. This poor man called, and the Lord heard him; he saved him out of all his troubles." (Psalms 34:5-6, NIV)*

SECTION FIVE

FAITH AND HEALING

Chapter Twenty-Two

FAITH

"Another part of dying to self is practicing your faith. Therefore, even when things seem dark, when there is no light around the corner you can see, when it seems as if you cannot even sense my presence, what glory you bring to me when you say, 'praise God and thank you Lord, for even though all seems dark, I put my trust in you.' Can you not see how the enemy would be defeated? How he would scatter as you exercise the faith that I have given you?"

"Trust in him at all times, O people; pour out your hearts to him, for God is our refuge." (Psalms 62:8, NIV)

"When you exercise your body, it grows lean, taut and powerful ...flab and fat turn to muscle...it is the same way with faith, trust and dying to self. It must be exercised to grow deeper and stronger.

"The ultimate victory is when difficult things happen; you can rejoice for others, as well as for yourself. You can uplift others when they have trials; you can hold your light aloft in a dark world.

"Go over your lesson on turning everything over to me, (see chapter on God's character) for when you truly understand it in your heart and when you understand what a merciful and loving Father I am, how truly you are loved, only then can you be a brilliant light for me.

"I have taught you about anger, fear and anxiety (see appropriate chapters). I want you all to be free of these things, for when you walk in freedom spiritually, you can see better, for your eyes are sharpened, you can hear better for your hearing will be more acute.

"I say to you all, well done good and faithful servant, well done. My gift to you is to set you free. Read over this lesson, ask me to help you glean what you need to learn. Praise me for I am a great God."

"You say, `I am rich; I have acquired wealth and do not need a thing.' But you do not realize that you are wretched, pitiful, poor, blind and naked."
(Revelation 3:17, NIV)

"Faith is a gift. It can be as small as a mustard seed. But like any seed that is planted, it needs water, sunlight and nourishment to grow. Each is intermingled to make it healthy.

"Water represents my word. You should read my word every day. Meditate on this and hide it in your hearts, know and feel the truth of it. Realize it is my Holy Spirit talking to you, guiding you in my will. For every problem you face, the answer is in my word.

"The sunlight is praising and worshiping me. I am worthy of praise. As you praise and worship me, great things happen. The spirit realm knows when it's happening. It fills my angels with joy and they join in praising me. I am faithful and just. A giving and loving Father. It pleases me to pour blessings down to restore you to the jewel-like essence you really are. Never forget to praise me. The seed of faith grows and grows.

"Nourishment comes from fellowshiping. Helping others, talking of me, sharing my love. If you do all these things, like praying continually, how could I not help but respond? My blessings start to flow, my oils pour down. My miracles start to happen as the seed of faith comes into full bloom.

"Throughout this growing time, there are many trials and tribulations. Some of my children are so overcome by adversity they go into shock. They stop reading the word, stop praising me, not understanding that the faith they need to sustain them could wither and die from such neglect. Yet those of you who persevere through these trials have many rewards. You become my vessels with many people looking at you with wonder and thinking, I wish I had faith like that or I wish I was so blessed. They can be blessed the same way. As any plant, faith must continually be watered, have sun and nourishment. Get this word into your heart. Practice it! You will be amazed at the rewards.

"Faith starts to give off-shoots of peace, serenity, wisdom and joy. The rewards of faith are mind boggling. All you need to begin is the faith of the mustard seed."

He replied, "Because you have so little faith. I tell you the truth, if you have faith as small as a mustard seed, you can say to this mountain, `Move from here to there' and it will move. Nothing will be impossible for you." (Matthew 17:20, NIV)

"Faith is like anything else, you must practice it. Exercise your faith in times of adversity, for adversity is your growing season. It is easy to sit back and thank me when the answer comes, but how I love to see you stand steadfast when the answer doesn't seem to be coming. That is when you must stand on my word, then your faith grows!

"When you tell people, 'it will be fun to sit back and watch what God does.' That is a faith statement. They are also a challenge to your flesh, for it is easy to believe in something you see, but it takes faith to believe in what you cannot see, without wavering.

"Faith, children, is all in what your desires are. Some pray without faith, without realizing I hear. But you become powerful instruments, when you pray with faith and with authority for you are of a royal line.

"You must desire me above all things, leaving the hurts aside. Lay them at my feet, lay also your burdens for I have paid for them... by my stripes you are healed. Apply this to adverse situations also. It does not mean healing physical and emotional problems alone, it can also mean the healing of a situation, a knitting and binding of a broken relationship. It can mean with the faith of a mustard seed you can all be as giants, my warriors and my intercessors. In so doing, you can stand claiming the scripture of, 'by my stripes you are healed,' for indeed, I am with you.

"Stand tall each of you, for I have gifted each with the spirit of faith. How it grows and develops is up to you."

A. ANXIOUS THOUGHTS

"Let no anxious thoughts come in, for therein is the victory. If you are nervous, before a speaking engagement, or before a sports event, claim and believe the scripture that says, 'I am your rear guard.' Claim and stand on the promise, when you call, I hear. Stand on the promise where two or more are gathered in my name, there am I. Seek and ye shall find, is another of my promises not utilized enough."

"He who dwells in the shelter of the Most High will rest in the shadow of the Almighty. I will say of the LORD, "He is my refuge and my fortress, my God, in whom I trust." (Psalms 91:1-2, NIV)

"You seek my will, then go about doing your own. If you truly seek my will, my answer, or my wisdom it will come to you whatever you request. It is then up to you whether you proceed with my will or not."

"Finally, be strong in the Lord and in his mighty power." (Ephesians 6:10, NIV)

"Too many are afraid of the unknown, too many when they are called to do something by me, say I will Lord, but later. Putting your trust and faith in me means just that. Not when its convenient for you, but every day.

"Every time there is a decision to be made, if you will stop and think, what would Jesus wish me to do? Will this bring shame or will it bring God glory? Do I really need this or not? Search my word to know what you should do. Seek my direction in prayer to make the right choice. If these steps are taken, how can you be anxious? How can you not have peace and tranquility?"

"Cast all your anxiety on him because he cares for you." (1 Peter 5:7, NIV)

"Meditate on this, for there is much to be gleaned."

"Remain in me, and I will remain in you. No branch can bear fruit by itself; it must remain in the vine. Neither can you bear fruit unless you remain in me. I am the vine; you are the branches. If a man remains in me and I in him, he will bear much fruit; apart from me you can do nothing. If anyone does not remain in me, he is like a branch that is thrown away and withers; such branches are picked up, thrown into the fire and burned. If you remain in me and my words remain in you, ask whatever you wish, and it will be given you." (John 15:4-7, NIV)

B. ATTITUDES

"Attitudes are like webs, they are elusive and so thin you can hardly see them. Dust the corners of your minds, sweep and bring to light any web of ignorance, blasphemy or bigotry."

"If we endure, we will also reign with him. If we disown him, he will also disown us." (2 Timothy 2:12, NIV)

"My spirit does a spiritual housecleaning and cleanses the cobwebs of your mind."

"He will sit as a refiner and purifier of silver; he will purify the Levites and refine them like gold and silver. Then the LORD will have men who will bring offerings in righteousness." (Malachi 3:3, NIV)

"Ask me each day to bring to light, any dark thoughts, any cobwebs. I want everyone dusted and polished for my return. I want you prepared. So says, your Lord."

"Search me, O God, and know my heart; test me and know my anxious thoughts. See if there is any offensive way in me, and lead me in the way everlasting." (Psalms 139:23-24, NIV)

"Trust in the LORD with all your heart and lean not on your own understanding; in all your ways acknowledge him, and he will make your paths straight." (Proverbs 3:5-6, NIV)

"For God did not give us a spirit of timidity, but a spirit of power, of love and of self-discipline." (2 Timothy 1:7, NIV)

C. ABIDING

"As your Father, your creator, and as the one who disciplines, loves, exhorts, sets free, polishes and refines, do you think you can trust me enough to abide in me?"

"Abiding in me gives such peace, pleasure and contentment. It will take a special abiding to meet the tasks and the trials for the end times. Abiding in me will keep your lamps well lit. Abiding in me opens your spiritual ears to hear what I am telling you and takes the blinders off your eyes. Oh little ones, to abide in me is the closest of walks. It is a place of joy unspeakable where no circumstance can penetrate. It is a place all should try to achieve."

"As for you, the anointing you received from him remains in you, and you do not need anyone to teach you. But as his anointing teaches you about all things and as that anointing is real, not counterfeit—just as it has taught you, remain in him. And now, dear children, continue in him, so that when he appears we may be confident and unashamed before him at his coming." **(1 John 2:27-28, NIV)**

"How can you learn this? By knowing me. To truly know me you have to love me. It is all intertwined. Beware of the chords of doubt, guilt and lukewarmness. These are the chords that strangle your righteous walk, these are the chords that seed discord and disbelieve. Ask me always to search your hearts."

"In that day you will no longer ask me anything. I tell you the truth, my Father will give you whatever you ask in my name. Until now you have not asked for anything in my name. Ask and you will receive, and your joy will be complete." **(John 16:23-24, NIV)**

D. ENDURANCE

"Patience and long suffering go hand in hand. Patience is an offshoot of faith; longsuffering and endurance are an offshoot of trust."

"Therefore, since we are surrounded by such a great cloud of witnesses, let us throw off everything that hinders and the sin that so easily entangles, and let us run with perseverance the race marked out for us." **(Hebrews 12:1, NIV)**

"Faith and trust go hand in hand."

"Being strengthened with all power according to his glorious might so that you may have great endurance and patience, and joyfully." **(Colossians 1:11, NIV)**

"So it is with the Christian walk. When there is trust, faith, growth and stamina you can go on. When there is little trust and faith, beware! For your walk can shrivel and die and you can return to the kingdom of darkness.

"Trust and faith should be the combined goal of everyone. For with them comes peace, tranquility and the chance for endurance. Endurance is the test of the Christian walk: endurance through criticism, endurance through hardships, endurance through misfortune, but with your eyes locked on me.

"As your faith and trust grows, so your endurance stretches. The chaff is being sifted from the wheat. The chaff are those faint-hearted people who never really knew me, or when their trials came, they could not endure.

"Endurance and long suffering is a goal you should strive to reach. It can be attained through trust and faith. They are all intermingled. That is why babes must be milk-fed and carefully guided through the pit falls, gently nurtured until their understanding blossoms. As you mature, more and more is expected of you. Endurance, like anything else worthwhile, is worth pursuing, praying for, and desiring."

"Let us draw near to God with a sincere heart in full assurance of faith, having our hearts sprinkled to cleanse us from a guilty conscience and having our bodies washed with pure water. Let us hold unswervingly to the hope we profess, for he who promised is faithful." (Hebrews 10:22-23, NIV)

"When you have endurance, you can go through any test, because you know your reward is beyond it; your reward will be for eternity. Endurance is kin with perseverance. It is a stubborn love and loyalty to me. A loyalty unwavering, a loyalty that endures any test.

"Endurance will see your prayers answered, ten, or fifteen years later. Many of my saints pray for the salvation of their loved ones for years, never losing faith. That is an endurance that brings reward. For those that do this have the faith that can move mountains. Endurance can also come in tests. Many miss the blessing because they give up, they do not persevere, they do not endure."

> *"And let us consider how we may spur one another on towards love and good deeds. Let us not give up meeting together, as some are in the habit of doing, but let us encourage one another—and all the more as you see the Day approaching."* **(Hebrews 10:24-25, NIV)**

"Endurance is a blessed assurance of my saving grace."

E. WAITING ON THE LORD

"Waiting on me requires trust and faith."

> *"But if we hope for what we do not yet have, we wait for it patiently."* **(Romans 8:25, NIV)**

"Trust that I am who I say I am. The God of creation, the healer, your banner, the Father of love. When I am secure in your hearts and you are grounded in the word, then waiting upon me is met with anticipation, joy and expectancy. Coupled with faith, waiting on me becomes as natural as breathing. Never forget, the prayers of a righteous man availeth much. Waiting on me for a word, a healing, a revelation, or knowledge always leads to the gifts of patience, peace and serenity."

> *"Wait for the LORD and keep his way. He will exalt you to inherit the land; when the wicked are cut off, you will see it."* **(Psalms 37:34, NIV)**

"Can you not see? You read my word daily to get it into your hearts and that is the groundwork. That in turn, leads to the inner knowledge of who I am. It becomes so unshakable that you are victors in standing firm; which leads to faith that can move mountains. Never forget, I am faithful, just, merciful and kind. As you wait on me, it can be a stretching of faith that becomes so second nature to you, you can surmount any obstacle."

"My children, know and understand with each tribulation you go through, I am with you. I turn all events to good through each trial. Waiting for my word, you grow in me."

"I wait for the LORD, my soul waits, and in his word I put my hope." **(Psalms 130:5, NIV)**

F. PRAYER

"Prayer and faith are my divine intervention tools. I use it to change lives, events and to bring forth healing. I also use prayers to put forth my good works and my desire or my will."

"I will instruct you and teach you in the way you should go; I will counsel you and watch over you." **(Psalms 32:8, NIV)**

"When you exercise faith and pray in earnest, steadfast and stalwart in the knowledge that I hear, what a weapon you have. Many do not realize the full extent of this power. When you pray and exercise your faith and what you ask is in my will, what can stop the answer? Know I inhabit the praises of my people. I am there when you search for me; I am there when you yearn for me; I am there when you beg my divine intervention. Only you, when you entertain doubts, when you wonder if I hear or pray without faith, stops me from acting on your behalf."

"Devote yourselves to prayer, being watchful and thankful." **(Colossians 4:2, NIV)**

"Satan has used lies, like 'you're not worthwhile,' 'who are you for God to hear?' for so long, that it takes a true knowledge of me to understand that prayer, with faith, is mighty.

"Satan never plays fair. He and his cohorts long to make you miserable. He laughs at your tears and feels victory when you doubt. When he can no longer attack you as a person, he attacks your children, spouses, anything and anyone he can use to cause you discomfort and to try to shake your faith. But I tell you, he is already defeated. I am mightier and I hold all in the palm of my hand. Commit your families to me, wash them in the blood daily, do spiritual warfare for them with the knowledge that demons will have to flee."

"This is the confidence we have in approaching God: that if we ask anything according to his will, he hears us. "And if we know that he hears us—whatever we ask—we know that we have what we asked of him."
(1 John 5:14-15, NIV)

"This is a testimony to my strength. Do battle, for you have the weapons you need. Stand in faith."

"Finally, be strong in the Lord and in his mighty power." (Ephesians 6:10, NIV)

"Prayer, with faith, like anything else, is to be used, used, and used. Note how often your prayers are answered. Note how often I answer other's prayers. Note I still work miracles. I still am in the midst of you. I still intervene on your behalf. I am still the same, yesterday, today and forever. If I am for you, who is against you?

"Check with me daily so, you can have a clean heart. Repent of any evil thoughts. Yield your body, spirit and soul to me and pray with pureness of motive."

"Therefore confess your sins to each other and pray for each other so that you may be healed. The prayer of a righteous man is powerful and effective."
(James 5:16, NIV)

"Do not pray with evil intent. Check your motives when you pray. Do not pray half-heartedly but enter in prayer with faith, for your prayers are heard. I tell you if you yield yourselves entirely to me, have faith and are clean before me, then be prepared to see your prayers answered. Always keep in mind that my timing is not yours and I have a greater plan. I see how people can be touched through someone's suffering. You see in your worldly eyes. You only see in the natural. Yet remember, I turn evil into good and I know how many hearts will be touched through someone's suffering.

"Stand in faith!

G. FURTHER INSIGHTS

"Each person is used differently, each person uniquely. Some are in charge of ministries, some are used as prayer warriors, and some as intercessors, but the one thing they have in common is faith in me, combined with love. One is not loved more then another. One is not favored more then another."

"It was he who gave some to be apostles, some to be prophets, some to be evangelists, and some to be pastors and teachers." (Ephesians 4:11, NIV)

"There are times when you look at something, a project, a need, a child on drugs, the loss of a job and the answer seems monumental and very distant. Yet, know you have the answer already. The answer is deep inside of you, for I dwell inside."

"Whoever claims to live in him must walk as Jesus did." (1 John 2:6, NIV)

"Since I live there in your hearts, is there anything I cannot do? It says in my word, seek and ye shall find, also, where two or more are gathered there am I in your midst.

Well, think about it. Think and focus your spirit eyes on the meaning. It means, if you have the faith for an answer (if it is in my will) it will be answered. It means I hear your prayers and you must exercise the faith of a mustard seed. Like anything else, you must practice. When you give all things to me, it is an act of faith. When you pray a request and believe, it is an act of faith. With practice, in the act of faith, you will grow stronger until you can say to that mountain, 'move' and it will."

> *"Let us draw near to God with a sincere heart in full assurance of faith, having our hearts sprinkled to cleanse us from a guilty conscience and having our bodies washed with pure water. Let us hold unswervingly to the hope we profess, for he who promised is faithful. And let us consider how we may spur one another on towards love and good deeds. Let us not give up meeting together, as some are in the habit of doing, but let us encourage one another—and all the more as you see the Day approaching."*
> *(Hebrews 10:22-25, NIV)*

"As you walk closer to me, as you daily lift your life to me, as you daily ask your petitions, rest easy 'little children,' for they are heard. My time is not yours. If you pray for a child on drugs, there may be deeper healing to take place before a deliverance of drugs can take place. Or the child may have to be brought to the point that he turns to me and me alone, forsaking all others and looking only to me."

> *"And he passed in front of Moses, proclaiming, "The LORD, the LORD, the compassionate and gracious God, slow to anger, abounding in love and faithfulness."* *(Exodus 34:6, NIV)*

"WHAT AM I TELLING YOU ABOUT FAITH?

"I am telling you to exercise faith and trust. That you cannot just mouth your prayers; truly mean them and know I will hear. You are not to allow doubt, fear, guilt, or anxious thoughts to stop me from working on your behalf. You are to persevere with long suffering. Stand in faith!

"I also tell you I love you and listen to your prayers when prayed with a pure heart. Always remember to have the faith of a mustard seed and you can move mountains.

"I am a God of love, and I see the greater plan; therefore, you must always pray in accordance with my will."

> *"Who of you by worrying can add a single hour to his life?" (Matthew 6:27, NIV)*

> *"Cast your cares on the LORD and he will sustain you; he will never let the righteous fall." (Psalms 55:22, NIV)*

See scripture **John 14:13.**

Chapter
Twenty-Three

HEALING—MOTIVES

"I deal with motives. I see not as you see. Focus your spirit eyes, look into yourselves, examine your motives, that is what I am saying. Let all things be to my glory.

"Check your hearts back through childhood for unrepented sins, for unrepented motives."

"Forgive us our sins, for we also forgive everyone who sins against us. And lead us not into temptation." **(Luke 11:4, NIV)**

"You see carnally my children, that which appears on the top, on the surface. But, I, dear children, see far deeper. I see the motive. Remember children, it is not just your works and your deeds which will be judged, but of far greater gravity is the judgment of your motive."

"Commit to the LORD whatever you do, and your plans will succeed." **(Proverbs 16:3, NIV)**

"To truly repent of sin is not just to repent of the act.

That is important, but equally important is to seek your motive for the act and ask me to forgive you of selfish or sinister motives.

"This is something that has been sorely neglected, yet it is something that will be judged. How much better children, if you repent now, rather then face me with that shame? Do you not see? I love you all so much, I will spare you that disgrace."

"For I will forgive their wickedness and will remember their sins no more." (Hebrews 8:12, NIV)

"Let's look at some examples so you can grasp the seriousness of motives."

A. ANGER: "You are irritable and snap at your mate, your friend, your fellow co-worker or anyone. You ask their forgiveness, you repent of your anger to me, but what was the motive? Were you upset because things were not going your way? Repent the motive of selfishness. Did you snap at them because they were not going fast enough for you or learning fast enough? Repent the motive of control. This can go on and on, but I say to you, check your motive."

"Be kind and compassionate to one another, forgiving each other, just as in Christ God forgave you." (Ephesians 4:32, NIV)

B. UNFORGIVENESS: "You repent and ask me to help you with unforgiveness, but what about help with your motive? Is it because of hurt or rejection? Repent of pride! Pride you ask? Yes, pride. Did my son not ask me to forgive them, they knew not what they do? Are you not my precious jewels? Are you not as precious to me as my Son was precious? Do you not see? Your reward is in heaven. What of the things man can do? It is nothing when you are going to spend eternity with me."

"Forgive us our debts, as we also have forgiven our debtors." (Matthew 6:12, NIV)

"Oh you of little faith. How much longer do I have to show you? How much longer do I have to reveal myself to you before you will harken?

"The day is coming soon, so evil, so filled with bile, that only you, my children can stand. Check your motives and understand the importance of this. So says, your Lord.

"If you check your motives, you will find as each motive is revealed and repented, the webbing or the bondage of the past will unravel. You are my children and as such, you are being shown the true meaning that those whom the Lord has set free, are free indeed."

"So, if the Son sets you free, you will be free indeed." (John 8:36, NIV)

"Do you not see? Oftentimes, my children continually repent of the same sin, trying hard to overcome it in my strength, when all the time, they had to but ask. 'What Lord is my motive in doing this?' This will bring forth healing and understanding as never before."

"For my thoughts are not your thoughts, neither are your ways my ways, declares the LORD." (Isaiah 55:8, NIV)

C. LYING: "Do you lie, or 'stretch the truth?' Ask me if your motive is fear and if so repent of it and ask me to set you free of it."

D. STEALING: Have you stolen? Repent of the motive of jealousy or pride. Not having what others have, or it could be a motive of trying to prove yourself and that also is pride.

E. OVEREATING, DRINKING, and SMOKING: Ask what the motive is here and repent of it's undealt anger, or addiction. Ask if it is a family curse passed down."

*"Let us behave decently, as in the daytime, not in orgies
and drunkenness, not in sexual immorality and
debauchery, not in dissension and jealousy."*
(Romans 13:13, NIV)

"What you are learning here is something few have been
able to grasp. Children, examine yourselves each day and
remember, repented sin and motive I throw into the sea of
forgetfulness."

*Then he adds: "Their sins and lawless acts I will
remember no more." (Hebrews 10:17, NIV)*

"I say to each and everyone of you. The time is short.
Who will there be? Who will still be praising me or praying
to me?

"Get your lives clean, while there is still time. So says,
the Lord."

Chapter
Twenty-Four

HEALING—FASTING

"I desire true love, not mediocre love. I desire faith, not fear. I desire truth, not lies. In each one of you, through the sins of your fathers, through sins of remission, through sins of unjust carnage, and carnality, there has been a separation. That is why I died, that is why I shed my blood. That is the bridge between truth and untruth, of freedom from despair into hope.

"At times, a fast is called to loosen the hold of demons either on your lives or the lives of others; to set you free from bondage and the yoke of despair. A fast is sometimes used to right yourself before me, to humble yourself.

"It is seldom used for repentance, for then it becomes a club. A fast should be entered into with joy, with prayer, with quietness and not with fanfare. The power of fasting has been underestimated. It is mighty to the pulling down of strongholds, it releases the new man and helps the old man to die, it releases from bondage, what otherwise would have remained entrenched."

"Finally, be strong in the Lord and in his mighty power." (Ephesians 6:10, NIV)

"Not only am I the great provider, but also a loving, nurturing Father. My Son died for you so you can live to glorify me. Many will falter and weaken. Those of you who persevere, those of you who continue to sing praises, raising Holy hands, have a place prepared for you.

"Yea, tho' you walk through the shadow of death, yea tho' you walk through financial disaster, yea tho' you walk through ill health, or slander, count it all joy. For I am not only able to deliver you, I will give you a peace and joy as you surrender your circumstances to my perfect will.

"My word says, seek and ye shall find, ask and it shall be given to you. Know that all things not only work for my glory, but for your own good. Many of you are called to go through trials that would cause the worldly to falter, shrivel, shake and die, yet, I will uphold you. I will shield you and give you peace that surpasses all understanding, enabling you to face any kind of adversity with joy!

"Many of the worldly see how you go through these tests. Many want to know, how you keep pressing onwards. Take this opportunity to witness my love; let my light shine through you so men will know me.

"Those of you who give so much of yourselves to help others, I say to you, 'it shall be returned to you, pressed down, shaken together and overflowing.'

"Adversity in the life of my children becomes a growing, stretching, testing and purifying time. Many of you who succumb to illness, while singing and praising me, will get the reward of the martyrs.

"Do not be discouraged, little ones, Satan is always unleashing his all, but my spirit is also pouring forth. Keep your eyes upon me, for I come soon. Look to all things as an opportunity to glorify me. That is your goal, to glorify the Father.

"Worthy is the lamb, for He died for you. His return is imminent...be prepared."

"But he [was] wounded for our transgressions, [he was] bruised for our iniquities: the chastisement of our peace [was] upon him; and with his stripes we are healed." **(Isaiah 53:5, NIV)**

Read **Ephesians 6:10-13**

Chapter Twenty-Five

HEALING— A CLEANSING

"He himself bore our sins in his body on the tree, so that we might die to sins and live for righteousness; by his wounds you have been healed." (1 Peter 2:24, NIV)

"When you claim this scripture, claim it with authority for, as my lambs, you are entitled to all the promises in my word, one of which is...by my stripes, you are healed.

"I would have you meditate on the fact that every lash I took, I took for you. As my blood spilled, it spilled for you. My blood is so pure that claiming it can bring healing to those who truly have and understand this principle in their spirits. My stripes are for healing and my death for salvation.

"Can you envision something so pure and clean it shone, being converged on by all the filth and dirt of sin? Then you will be able to see the paradox, not only of the shedding of my blood and my death but of a death that can be claimed for healing. I have shown you that sinners nailed and crucified me, trying to shut out my light, yet nothing can stop the power of my blood or my lashings."

> *"My son, pay attention to what I say; listen closely to my words. Do not let them out of your sight, keep them within your heart; for they are life to those who find them and health to a man's whole body."*
> *(Proverbs 4:20-22, NIV)*

"It is never my desire you have illnesses, yet I can use illness and turn it into good. Never forget, I see the heart. I know the needs of mankind."

> *"As he went along, he saw a man blind from birth. His disciples asked him, "Rabbi, who sinned, this man or his parents, that he was born blind?" "Neither this man nor his parents sinned," said Jesus, "but this happened so that the work of God might be displayed in his life." (John 9:1-2, NIV)*

"My children, it takes faith and understanding that, 'by my stripes you are healed.' Often these words are just mouthed, but if you can get the dynamics and power of what's being said into your spirits, then and only then, can it be used effectively."

> *"But he was pierced for our transgressions, he was crushed for our iniquities; the punishment that brought us peace was upon him, and by his wounds we are healed." (Isaiah 53:5, NIV)*

"Know I did not leave you defenseless. I did not leave you without weapons. You have the armor, spirit discernment, my blood for protection and my stripes for healing.

"My blood, being so pure, was spilled to take all your sins, including the sins of illness. If you can get this into your spirits, you have a powerful tool, a tool of faith, a tool as powerful as spiritual discernment.

"Claiming this scripture with full authority, given to you by me, means you do not have to accept illnesses or curses of family illness passed down from generation to generation. Claim this with the understanding that it is also a powerful tool of spiritual warfare.

"My warriors, arm yourselves with all the weapons I have given you and understand the defenses I have given you. Claim these with the faith of a child and it will be so.

"There is so little time left. My daughters and sons, you must unite in prayer and know the power I have given you. Stand on my word! Stand firm in time of adversity and know you will soon be in glory with me.

"Prepare! Lift yourselves daily in prayer. My spirit pours forth, utilize it. So says, your Lord."

"Look upon my affliction and my distress and take away all my sins." (Psalms 25:18, NIV)

SECTION SIX

INSIGHTS INTO
CHRISTIAN LIVING

Chapter
Twenty-Six

EVANGELICALS AND
OTHER CHRISTIANS

"I have many mansions in my kingdom. Some of my saints will receive crowns and rewards. It is not as the flesh sees, but as the spirit sees."

> *"In my Father's house are many rooms; if it were not so, I would have told you. I am going there to prepare a place for you."* **(John 14:2, NIV)**

"Since I see into the heart, would it not stand to reason that I see the intentions of your thoughts and heart? Of course I would."

> *"If we confess our sins, he is faithful and just and will forgive us our sins and purify us from all unright - eousness."* **(1 John 1:9, NIV)**

"Who is to say who I love more? Does it say anywhere in my word this is so? Yet those of you who are in my battle, will receive rewards and blessings."

"Since you know that you will receive an inheritance from the Lord as a reward. It is the Lord Christ you are serving." (Colossians 3:24, NIV)

"Thinking you are a special people has caused numerous problems throughout the centuries. You are blessed because you have listened for my voice, you are blessed because of the sweet communion.

"The only way to show my light is through love and an inner joy. People will be drawn to you as a moth to flame.

"You do and will receive extra blessings, but be careful my children not to get puffed up or swelled up with pride because you hear my voice."

"You need to persevere so that when you have done the will of God, you will receive what he has promised." (Hebrews 10:36, NIV)

"I also guide many of my sons and daughters, they are just not aware of it. All my children are not ready for close communion with me; it does not make them less dear."

"A new command I give you: Love one another. As I have loved you, so you must love one another." (John 13:34, NIV)

"Take this to heart, evangelical or charismatic is not the only way to me, yet for many it is the right way.

"Be careful when you call yourselves Christians, that you act as Christians. The eyes of many are on you. As long as you ask for my guidance all will be well. Get these thoughts into your heart."

"Therefore, as we have opportunity, let us do good to all people, especially to those who belong to the family of believers." (Galatians 6:10, NIV)

"Always walk the road of love, joining your brothers and sisters of other denominations in prayer and supplication.

Pray for your country, pray for your homes, pray for my spirit to pour forth. Uphold each other. Rather than argue a difference in your theology, join together praising the Father, Son and Holy Spirit. This is my church. This is my church of love, one for another. Meditate on this."

"By this all men will know that you are my disciples, if you love one another." (John 13:35, NIV)

Chapter Twenty-Seven

OBEDIENCE

You can be in obedience by:

A. DESIRING GUIDANCE.

"Desiring it enough to stay in my word, desiring it to the extent of wanting it as much as life itself. Obedience to me, is in reality, "dying to self." Walking in obedience to me, is laying your 'self' down over each and every desire and seeking my will. You can come to this place if you so desire. It is the same as when I said, leave all your earthly possessions, and follow me. I say to you, leave all your fleshly desires and follow me. One is intermingled with the other. If you give me all your earthly treasures, and it does not take precedence over me, then understand I don't desire them, but desire your willingness to give them up if I should ask. That is walking in obedience."

"Dear friends, if our hearts do not condemn us, we have confidence before God and receive from him anything

*we ask, because we obey his commands and do what
pleases him. And this is his command: to believe in
the name of his Son, Jesus Christ, and to love one
another as he commanded us. Those who obey his
commands live in him, and he in them. And this is how
we know that he lives in us: We know it by the Spirit he
gave us." (1 John 3:21-24, NIV)*

B. LOVE ONE ANOTHER, EVEN THE UNLOVABLE.

"I lived among the whores and the thieves, but I did not
seek out the Pharisees. So it is with loving one another,
carrying one another's burdens, even the unlovable.
Unlovable can be one who spitefully talks of you; unlovable
can be one who is impolite; unlovable can be one who is
intolerant. Each of these things needs prayer. Not
judgement, not condemnation, but love, and prayer. That is
loving one another."

*"For just as through the disobedience of the one man
the many were made sinners, so also through the obe -
dience of the one man the many will be made
righteous. The law was added so that the trespass
might increase. But where sin increased, grace
increased all the more, so that, just as sin reigned in
death, so also grace might reign through righteousness
to bring eternal life through Jesus Christ our Lord."
(Romans 5:19-21, NIV)*

C. SUBMITTING ONE TO ANOTHER.

"This is the way of the humble heart. Humbleness is my
way. That is why I say, the least shall be first. It pertains to
humbleness. I washed my apostles' feet. I submitted to
them in love, in compassion. Defer one to another. If a
person is in charge of a ministry, one I have selected, it is
because their hearts are right for that job. Not only their
hearts, but their uniqueness. Many have been groomed for
ministries, since their birth.

"Being submissive does not mean to be a door mat, that is a perversion of my word. If you have fought with your brother, go to him in love, in submissiveness, allowing the humbleness not only to show through but to be ingrained in you. Yielding, deferring one to another, in love, leads to peace and unity of spirit. That is heavenly obedience on earth."

"In everything set them an example by doing what is good. In your teaching show integrity, seriousness and soundness of speech that cannot be condemned, so that those who oppose you may be ashamed because they have nothing bad to say about us. Teach slaves to be subject to their masters in everything, to try to please them, not to talk back to them, and not to steal from them, but to show that they can be fully trusted, so that in every way they will make the teaching about God our Savior attractive." (Titus 2:7-10, NIV)

D. PRAY WITHOUT CEASING IT'S THE WILL OF GOD

"This does not mean you have to be on your knees all the time. If you seek my will over yours, if you love one another, if you defer to one another, you are walking closer and closer to me and therefore you will be rejoicing all the time. That is a form of praying. I love to hear my people praise me, for I am a just and merciful God. When you have supplications, when you have desires, when you have needs, when you travail one for another, I am right there in the midst of you. If I am right there, my power is there also, my healing powers can flow, healing broken relationships, healing bodies. I hear your prayers for intervention of my mercy and **you will be heard** because you are walking in obedience, walking in love, yielding one to another."

"Therefore confess your sins to each other and pray for each other so that you may be healed. The prayer of a righteous man is powerful and effective." (James 5:16, NIV)

E. TRAVAIL ONE FOR ANOTHER.

"This means carrying one another's burdens and lifting them up to me in prayer. If you pray without ceasing and lift others to me constantly, then the self dies. If the self dies, you are walking in obedience.

"Know, little ones, all this is attainable. Know if you do this, there will be a great freeing. The freeing comes because you walk in obedience, humbleness, love and yielding one to another. If you are faithful in this, how can worry enter, even in the direst of circumstances? How can anxiety take hold? It can bring peace, for you no longer carry burdens, but daily give them to me."

"Who of you by worrying can add a single hour to his life?" (Matthew 6:27, NIV)

"And pray in the Spirit on all occasions with all kinds of prayers and requests. With this in mind, be alert and always keep on praying for all the saints." (Ephesians 6:18, NIV)

"When you seek, so shall you find and this I say to you. I bless you for desiring these things."

"Ask and it will be given to you; seek and you will find; knock and the door will be opened to you." (Matthew 7:7, NIV)

"I love those who love me, and those who seek me find me." (Proverbs 8:17, NIV)

"It is a formula to a trouble free life. Not from adversity but that even in adversity, you can rejoice. Your "spirit eyes" will come into such sharp focus, that you will be able to see beyond the circumstances and see my plan. My plans always have eternity, and salvation at the crux of them."

Chapter Twenty-Eight

JUDGING

"Judging your fellow Christians, judging anyone, anywhere, is something you must all take care not to do. Judging can bring pride, such as 'I would never do a thing like that.' It allows Satan to work over time to make you so prideful you cannot see what you must see. The Pharisees studied the law, but did not live by it. When they fasted, they did it for all to see. They lived without compromise for anyone else's sin, hiding their own."

"Woe to you, teachers of the law and Pharisees, you hypocrites! You clean the outside of the cup and dish, but inside they are full of greed and self-indulgence."
(Matthew 23:25, NIV)

"When one judges another, do you not see? If it is not with love, if it is without compassion or kindness, it will turn the one sinning away from me, because of your own self righteousness."

> *"Do not judge, or you too will be judged. For in the*
> *same way as you judge others, you will be judged, and*
> *with the measure you use, it will be measured to*
> *you.'Why do you look at the speck of sawdust in your*
> *brother's eye and pay no attention to the plank in your*
> *own eye? How can you say to your brother, `Let me*
> *take the speck out of your eye,' when all the time there*
> *is a plank in your own eye? You hypocrite, first take*
> *the plank out of your own eye, and then you will see*
> *clearly to remove the speck from your brother's eye."*
> *(Matthew 7:1-5, NIV)*

"Judging is an abhorrence to me. It leads the person who is being judged, as well as the one doing the judging, to be held accountable on Judgment Day. Oh, afflicted ones, how long before I come? Are you ready?

"The harm over judging cannot be stressed enough. There are many who I was gently leading, when someone in self righteousness said to them, 'Well, if you believed as you say you do, you wouldn't be smoking or drinking.' Don't you see the condemnation that heaps on a person? My spirit draws them slowly, gently with love until these things are gone from their lives. What is more important? Someone not smoking or drinking or **their soul?**"

> *"So when you, a mere man, pass judgment on them and*
> *yet do the same things, do you think you will escape*
> *God's judgment? Or do you show contempt for the*
> *riches of his kindness, tolerance and patience, not*
> *realizing that God's kindness leads you towards*
> *repentance?" (Romans 2:3-4, NIV)*

"Remember when I came into your lives? Were any of you perfect? Did not and do not each of you still have things to be taken out of your lives? Give another the same chance, but pray for them.

"It is the same with prayer requests. Take care, when you put in a request for another person it is not in gossip. Example: Let's pray for so and so, you know he is drinking.

When you uncover another person, make sure your motive is pure and the person praying with you is discreet."

> *"For everyone who exalts himself will be humbled, and he who humbles himself will be exalted." (Luke 14:11, NIV)*

"There are times, when there is a sin that has to be confronted. The best way to handle that is to go to the pastor and pray with him. If he agrees, take a sister or brother in Christ, to gently with love, confront the person. If there is no repentance, then dust your feet, yet keep them in prayer."

> *"So they shook the dust from their feet in protest against them and went to Iconium." (Acts 13:51, NIV)*

"I warn you all. Take care on this step, that you do not act out of hurt or vengeance. Always remember it is in my words to love your enemy.

"You are to judge words that are given in prophecy. However I warn you, judge the word not who gives it. How you judge, so shall I judge you."

> *"Do not judge, and you will not be judged. Do not condemn, and you will not be condemned. Forgive, and you will be forgiven." (Luke 6:37, NIV)*

> *"For everyone who exalts himself will be humbled, and he who humbles himself will be exalted." (Luke 14:11, NIV)*

> *"But if we judged ourselves, we would not come under judgment. When we are judged by the Lord, we are being disciplined so that we will not be condemned with the world." (1 Corinthians 11:31-32, NIV)*

Chapter Twenty-Nine

LONGSUFFERING

"Learn that long suffering is not meant as a drudgery, but as a lifestyle of putting your cares at my feet. Do you not see? When you say Lord, not my will, but yours be done, it is a way of long suffering, enduring anything with tolerance and forbearance because you know I never give more than can be endured. I always have a door open when one closes. I will not let you fall. If I am for you, who is against you."

"But the fruit of the Spirit is love, joy, peace, patience, kindness, goodness, faithfulness." (Galatians 5:22, NIV)

"You see, long suffering brings stronger faith and with that strong faith comes an unshakable peace.

"Long suffering is not natural but spiritual. It comes from faith and asking me to help you to be long suffering. It is an unmovable, unflappable direction and a road my apostles knew well."

"Not only so, but we also rejoice in our sufferings, because we know that suffering produces perseverance."
(Romans 5:3, NIV)

"Long suffering is what helps you get over grief. Long suffering is what love is. (Slow to anger, always looking for my answers when all else fails.) Long suffering defeats doubt."

"In purity, understanding, patience and kindness; in the Holy Spirit and in sincere love." (2 Corinthians 6:6, NIV)

"It is not a martyrdom, but a positive life style, a walking in sure knowledge of me; a letting go of your flesh and allowing me to become more. It is a way through the refiners fire. It is a way to peace and joy in your life. It is a way of living spiritually in a carnal world.

"If you get anything into your hearts, let it be this, long suffering does not mean going around with a long face, suffering untold injustices. It is a willingness to believe that your rewards are truly in heaven."

"Therefore, as God's chosen people, holy and dearly loved, clothe yourselves with compassion, kindness, humility, gentleness and patience." (Colossians 3:12, NIV)

"If you cry out to me to help you defeat intolerance in your life, as well as the evil surrounding it, know it is my perfect will to defeat it in your life, and if it is my perfect will, will I not only equip you to defeat it, but uplift and uphold you to defeat it?"

"Finally, be strong in the Lord and in his mighty power." (Ephesians 6:10, NIV)

"It is the same with temperance, what is the opposite of temperance? It is an addictive nature! A life run riot. One where there is no control in a given situation. One of lustful disposition. Example: alcoholism, drug addiction, promiscuity, spending money, religiosity and overeating.

"Do you not see? Your life without temperance leads you into, or back into, Satan's territory. I would have you ask me if there is an area in your life you lack temperance, or if there is an area in your life you need healed, or an area in your life you need deliverance.

"Remember, *"Then you will know the truth, and the truth will set you free." (John 8:32 NIV).* If that is so, does it not stand to reason I wish to set all free, and that is in every area of your lives?

"Take time to meditate on this, and realize that there will be a freeing, there will be a healing, if you but ask.

"Know you have each been chosen, for I have first loved you. You are my emissaries as well as my light in this dark world. Take advantage of this time for healing and setting free."

"But you are a chosen people, a royal priesthood, a holy nation, a people belonging to God, that you may declare the praises of him who called you out of darkness into his wonderful light. Once you were not a people, but now you are the people of God; once you had not received mercy, but now you have received mercy. " Dear friends, I urge you, as aliens and strangers in the world, to abstain from sinful desires, which war against your soul."
(1 Peter 2:9-11, NIV)

"I have been crucified with Christ and I no longer live, but Christ lives in me. The life I live in the body, I live by faith in the Son of God, who loved me and gave himself for me." (Galatians 2:20, NIV)

Chapter Thirty

HUMBLENESS

"Christian humility is that grace which makes one think of himself no more highly than he ought to think."

For by the grace given me I say to every one of you: Do not think of yourself more highly than you ought, but rather think of yourself with sober judgment, in accordance with the measure of faith God has given you. (Romans 12:3, NIV)

"It requires you to feel that in God's sight you have no merit, and an honor to prefer our brethren to ourselves but does not demand undue self-depreciation or depressing views of one's self, but lowliness of self-estimation, freedom from vanity."

Be devoted to one another in brotherly love. Honour one another above yourselves. (Romans 12:10, NIV)

It is enjoined of God. (Colossians 3:12; James, 4:6)

"The word is equivalent to meekness and is essential to discipleship for Jesus Christ."

"He guides the humble in what is right and teaches them his way." (Psalms 25:9, NIV)

And he said: "I tell you the truth, unless you change and become like little children, you will never enter the kingdom of heaven. Therefore, whoever humbles himself like this child is the greatest in the kingdom of heaven." (Matthew 18:3-4, NIV)

"A false spirit of humility is just that...false, a burden placed on yourself to have humility and it is false because it is not from me. Remember, I see what is in the heart. Putting on a false front in an effort to impress people only adds to your burden of sin.

"False humility is not humbleness, so do not get it confused with humility. Humbleness is of me for I walked in it, I felt it and that is how my children shall walk."

"Do not let anyone who delights in false humility and the worship of angels disqualify you for the prize. Such a person goes into great detail about what he has seen, and his unspiritual mind puffs him up with idle notions." (Colossians 2:18, NIV)

"If my words on humility and humbleness confuse you, and you seek understanding, then know this. False humility is false because it is worldly. To humble yourself is in my word. As in everything else, false humility is a counterfeit of humbleness. False humility is not for my children, you never have to be humiliated.

"To be humble is to be meek, mild, unassuming, courteous to the point of putting others first."

"Therefore, as God's chosen people, holy and dearly loved, clothe yourselves with compassion, kindness, humility, gentleness and patience." (Colossians 3:12, NIV)

"When you have the spirit of humbleness, it brings peace and contentment because it is not difficult to put another person ahead of yourself and be truly peaceful... that is the crux of humbleness and that enables you to walk in love. False humility, on the other hand, is walking with eyes on yourself, not me, therefore, it is counterfeit."

"Such regulations indeed have an appearance of wisdom, with their self-imposed worship, their false humility and their harsh treatment of the body, but they lack any value in restraining sensual indulgence." **(Colossians 2:23, NIV)**

"There is a world of difference. Examine yourselves! If you have been walking in false humility, look at it for what it is. Let go of it and you are then free to walk in humbleness."

"For everyone who exalts himself will be humbled, and he who humbles himself will be exalted." **(Luke 14:11, NIV)**

"This is something few of my children can grasp, but if you ask me to open your eyes and your heart to this, there will come a deep understanding so you can have more freedom then ever before; freedom to walk in humbleness and therefore love. This is a lesson to be taken to heart. Learn this! I say to all of you, 'Well done, good and faithful servants.'"

Young men, in the same way be submissive to those who are older. All of you, clothe yourselves with humility towards one another, because, "God opposes the proud but gives grace to the humble." Humble yourselves, therefore, under God's mighty hand, that he may lift you up in due time." **(1 Peter 5:5-6, NIV)**

"To truly walk in humbleness it must come naturally from me within you; therefore, walking in false humility is

walking in your humanness; walking in humbleness is of
me. You are not to feel guilty if you have been walking in
false humility for most have been trying to please me,
searching to walk in the humbleness I tell you to. Yet, if you
relax, be yourself, worship me, give me your hearts, you
will start walking in humbleness. A humbleness so natural
it's like breathing because you will be open to it, open to my
spirit within you. Therefore, walking in humbleness will
come quite naturally as the love of the Lord grows in you."

*"But he gives us more grace. That is why Scripture
says: 'God opposes the proud but gives grace to the
humble.'" (James 4:6, NIV)*

Chapter Thirty-One

ENDURANCE

"See endurance in the chapter on faith and utilize it in dying to self."

"May the God who gives endurance and encouragement give you a spirit of unity among yourselves as you follow Christ Jesus," (Romans 15:5, NIV)

"Therefore, since we are surrounded by such a great cloud of witnesses, let us throw off everything that hinders and the sin that so easily entangles, and let us run with perseverance the race marked out for us." (Hebrews 12:1, NIV)

"let us draw near to God with a sincere heart in full assurance of faith, having our hearts sprinkled to cleanse us from a guilty conscience and having our bodies washed with pure water. Let us hold unswervingly to the hope we profess, for he who promised is faithful. And let us consider how we may spur one another on towards love and good deeds. Let us not give up meeting together, as some are in the habit of doing, but let us encourage one another—and all the more as you see the Day approaching. (Hebrews 10:22-25 ,NIV)

Chapter
Thirty-Two

PATIENCE

"I teach you patience. Patience is that calm and unruffled temper with which the good man bears the evils of life, whether they proceed from persons or things. It also manifests itself in a sweet submission to the providential appointments of God and fortitude in the presence of the duties and conflicts of life. This grace will save you from discouragement in the face of evil and will aid in the cultivation of godliness."

By standing firm you will gain life. (Luke 21:19, NIV)

"For this very reason, make every effort to add to your faith goodness; and to goodness, knowledge; and to knowledge, self-control; and to self-control, perseverance; and to perseverance, Godliness." (2 Peter 1:5-6, NIV)

"The development of the entire Christian character and, continued until the end, will terminate in reward, in the life to come."

"Perseverance must finish its work so that you may be mature and complete, not lacking anything."
(James 1:4, NIV)

"To those who by persistence in doing good seek glory, honour and immortality, he will give eternal life."
(Romans 2:7, NIV)

"Be patient, then, brothers, until the Lord's coming. See how the farmer waits for the land to yield its valuable crop and how patient he is for the autumn and spring rains. You too, be patient and stand firm, because the Lord's coming is near." (James 5:7-8, NIV)

"Patience for my return, patience for the end, patience for your families. I say to you, have I not waited for thousands of years for man to leave his idols, his wickedness, to come to me? You see, if I were impatient, many who are or will be saved, wouldn't have had the chance.

"The one thing that can help you with patience is: it is a privilege and a sacrifice to me. In that way, the waiting becomes more tolerable and as you overcome each little impatience in your life, you will find it is a joy, yes a joy, to wait."

"And to knowledge, self-control; and to self-control, perseverance; and to perseverance, godliness."
(2 Peter 1:6, NIV)

"Perseverance must finish its work so that you may be mature and complete, not lacking anything."
(James 1:4, NIV)

"To those who by persisting in doing good seek glory, honor and immortality, he will give eternal life."
(Romans 2:7, NIV)

"Be patient, then brothers, until the Lord's coming. See how the farmer waits for the land to yield its valuable crop and how patient he is for the autumn and spring rains. You too, be patient and stand firm, because the Lord's coming is near." (James 5:7-8, NIV)

Chapter Thirty-Three

JOY

"My child, in all things give thanks for it is my will. Know in your heart of hearts I would not harm you. When you give thanks, combined with joy what a tool that is. What a faith builder.

"Learn this and learn it well, each of you. If you ask me to do something in your lives, if you ask my hand to move and then you worry, say it is in Gods' hands, yet still anxiously look for the answer, where is the faith?"

"Who of you by worrying can add a single hour to his life?" (Matthew 6:27, NIV)

"He replied, Because you have so little faith. I tell you the truth, if you have faith as small as a mustard seed, you can say to this mountain, 'Move from here to there' and it will move. Nothing will be impossible for you." (Matthew 17:20, NIV)

"Faith like that is combined with joy and peace in the knowledge that I, your Lord God, desire all good things for you. Truly letting go and leaving all in my hands is just that. A calm, quiet assurance that indeed I will move or work in my time. Never forget, I have the victory already, never forget I turn evil to good, never forget to yield to my will, not yours."

"Your kingdom come, your will be done on earth as it is in heaven." (Matthew 6:10, NIV)

"Let everything you ask for in my name be asked unselfishly and in love. If it is not answered, get your spirit eyes in focus, for never forget, I see the greater plan. Sometimes tragedy that comes to you, can bring great blessings to many.

"Always give glory to me. Be thankful and joyful in your hearts for that is my gift to each of you. Joy dispels gloom, joy dissipates anxiety, joy breaks up anguish. Joy also brings forth forgiveness, and breaks the spirit of heaviness."

"Give thanks in all circumstances, for this is God's will for you in Christ Jesus." (1 Thessalonians 5:18, NIV)

"This is a deeper understanding of that scripture. Get this into your hearts and you have another key. A key to spiritual warfare so powerful, that Satan's priority is to steal your joy. Can you now understand why?

"Those of you who take these lessons to heart will grow and with that growth defeat the enemy, for you have true understanding of the weapons I have left you.

"Never forget to give all glory and honor to me, never forget to plead the blood over any situation. Never forget to say, your will not mine.

"Joy brings forth song, joy brings forth happiness. Take care in all adverse situations to know deep in your hearts, I will not let you fall. Then and only then can you learn this lesson, for it is to be shared."

"Consider it pure joy, my brothers, whenever you face trials of many kinds, because you know that the testing of your faith develops perseverance." **(James 1:2-3, NIV)**

"Always giving thanks to God the Father for everything, in the name of our Lord Jesus Christ."
(Ephesians 5:20, NIV)

Chapter
Thirty-Four

PRIDE

"The prideful nature of man is difficult at best to overcome. It is inherent to most of us and it stems from the 'let me, I can do it better syndrome.'

"In order for you to let the old nature die, and to relinquish the hold of the past, you must include your pride. In that way, you can truly relinquish your all to me. Relinquishing your all, or dying to self, is to be done each day. Lift yourselves in full humbleness to me."

"Humble yourselves, therefore, under God's mighty hand, that he may lift you up in due time." (1 Peter 5:6, NIV)

"Remember that I dwell inside you, and I see your thoughts. Do you now realize that I see not only your hearts, but your thoughts? Daily lift your thoughts to me. Daily ask for a clean heart. Daily repent of the previous days sins, start afresh.

"Pride is a lonely walk and a favorite plan of attack by the enemy. Practice what I have told you and all will be well. I keep you safe from harm. I surround you with my protection. Know that without me, there would be nothing. Without me there would be no sweetness to the victory for there would be no victory."

"I can do everything through him who gives me strength." (Philippians 4:13, NIV)

"Honor the Lord God, by submitting and turning over all areas of your life to me. Practicing will bring forth victory.

"This is a deep insight. Meditate on it, practice it and it will bring forth rewards beyond your dreams or your imagination. It will bring you my spirit of peace and tranquility. Many will not grasp the deeper meanings here, yet those who grasp them will be nourished."

"For sin shall not be your master, because you are not under law, but under grace." (Romans 6:14, NIV)

"Sometimes when the way seems dim, an unworthy thought or deed has gotten in the way. In order to keep my light brilliant and shining straight through to you, keep all areas of your life pure, so that, when any ungodly thoughts come into your mind, you recognize them right away and rebuke them. Most of you are still in the process of cleansing your thoughts and your mind, hence it is hard for you to distinguish, 'if' and 'where' you have gone wrong. I see all, even thoughts that surface uninvited to you, for I am your protector. You must willingly allow me to have full reign in your heart, body, soul and thoughts. There is spiritual housecleaning to do."

"Pride goes before destruction, a haughty spirit before a fall." (Proverbs 16:18, NIV)

"Judgement is the right of your Lord God alone, for I alone see true motives. There will be a judgement day for all. You will also be judged, all of you, on your good works, your kindness to others, and your forgiving nature. Stand tall! In order to do so, you must allow me to deal with the pride and judgement that you exercise. Once you see pride for what it is, a dark work, you will be able, not only to let go of it, but walk in humility and experience a freeing. Take care not to assume others think as you. Take care not to judge in the smallest degree. Remember, walk in compassion and love. Walking in forgiveness is just that, forgiving and forgetting."

"This is the Godly way I would have you walk. A way to me, the right way, the true way, so says your Lord."

Chapter Thirty-Five

OUR ROLES DEFINED BY GOD

"It must be remembered, everyone's path is and has been predestined. Some have wealth to further my kingdom, some have the intuitive instinct for working hard, being good parents and upright honest citizens.

"Some live in hell and after their deliverance are used to bring many people to me, their Lord. There are those that endure tragedy, financial ruin, have had bad health, or emotional upset, and they still praise me. Those are my martyrs. Which is more blessed? You see with worldly eyes and I see with spiritual eyes. Each person is equipped with the ability to walk and overcome his or her given circumstance. Some are evangelists, some prophets, some teachers. To whom much is given, much is expected. There are tests and trials, refining constantly being done. Heaven on earth is a close walk with me.

"Who is more blessed? None, for I love you all. Can a hand move without the arm? You see, each has his destiny."

"Rejoice, I give none, more than they can endure, who eat my people's flesh, strip off their skin and break their bones in pieces; who chop them up like meat for the pan, like flesh for the pot." (Micah 3:3, NIV)

"You were taught, with regard to your former way of life, to put off your old self, which is being corrupted by its deceitful desires; to be made new in the attitude of your minds; and to put on the new self, created to be like God in true righteousness and holiness. Therefore each of you must put off falsehood and speak truthfully to his neighbor, for we are all members of one body." (Ephesians 4:22-25, NIV)

Chapter Thirty-Six

CONCLUSION

"What do I say to one who has read this book?

"Hold fast to the truths you have read. My return is imminent. The evil one is stepping up his actions, his leading. There will be more rampant murders, for murder's sake. Innocents are being abused, molestation is on the rise and yet, I would have you, my people, stay in prayer, for I also am working. My spirit is going to be unleashed upon this world, as never before. Signs and wonders will occur. It will be the last great harvest.

"I say, get right before me. Stand your ground for decency, taking care Satan does not make you slip down to his level. I say to one and all, rejoice for I return soon. Though you are in tribulation, keep your eyes on me. In that way you can overcome the circumstances you will endure. Never lose faith, I protect my own. Never lose faith for you are my church. Arise, stand tall, victory through me will come."

"For this reason, since the day we heard about you, we have not stopped praying for you and asking god to fill you with the knowledge of his will through all spiritual wisdom and understanding. And we pray this in order that you may live a life worthy of the Lord and may please him in every way: bearing fruit in every good work, growing in the knowledge of God, being strengthened with all power according to his glorious might so that you may have great endurance and patience, and joyfully giving thanks to the Father, who has qualified you to share in the inheritance of the saints in the kingdom of light. for he has rescued us from the dominion of darkness and brought us into the kingdom of the Son he loves;" **(Colossians 1:9-13, NIV)**

"Nations are in uproar, kingdoms fall; he lifts his voice, the earth melts. The Lord Almighty is with us; the God of Jacob is our fortress. Selah Come and see the works of the Lord, the desolations he has brought on the earth. He makes wars cease to the ends of the earth; he breaks the bow and shatters the spear, he burns the shields with fire. Be still and know that I am God; I will be exalted among the nations, I will be exalted in the earth." **(Psalms 46:6-10, NIV)**

"Now the Lord is the Spirit, and where the Spirit of the Lord is, there is freedom." **(2 Corinthians 3:17, NIV)**